Green Peak
Olympus Guard Station (summer only)
Five Mile Island Camp
800 Trail
Hoh
River
River
Cougar Cr
Mount
Tom
5016
5121

FAST MOVING WATER

Images and Essays from the Hoh River

Photography by Keith Lazelle

Documentary Media
Seattle, Washington

Fast Moving Water
Images and Essays from the Hoh River

Published by Documentary Media
3250 41st Ave SW
Seattle, WA 98116
(206) 935-9292
books@docbooks.com
www.documentarymedia.com

First edition 2008
Printed in China

Photographer: Keith Lazelle Nature Photography
Project Manager: Phil Davis
Contributing Sponsor: Western Rivers Conservancy
Editorial Director: Petyr Beck
Editor: Judy Gouldthorpe
Publisher: Barry Provorse
Cover Design: Paul Langland Design

Library of Congress Cataloging-in-Publication Data
Lazelle, Keith D.
Fast moving water : images and essays from the Hoh River / photography by Keith Lazelle. -- 1st ed.
p. cm.

ISBN 978-1-933245-10-2
1. Hoh River (Wash.)--Pictorial works. 2. Hoh River Valley (Wash.)--Pictorial works.
3. Hoh River (Wash.)--Description and travel. 4. Hoh River Valley (Wash.)--Description and travel.
5. Natural history--Washington (State)--Hoh River Valley. 6. Hoh River Valley (Wash.)--History.
7. Hoh River Valley (Wash.)--Social life and customs. 8. River life--Washington (State)--
Hoh River Valley. 9. Community life--Washington (State)--Hoh River Valley. I. Title.

F897.H63L39 2008
979.7'9800222--dc22
2007050539

Contents

Foreword

by Representative Norm Dicks

Of all the great many natural treasures in the state of Washington, and I believe that my Congressional District—the Sixth—has the most, the Hoh River is a crown jewel. The Hoh is a place of legends: the most rainfall of any place on the continent, the finest rain forest in the country, the strongest salmon runs in the Northwest, the biggest steelhead in the state, the proudest pioneer heritage on the Olympic Peninsula, and perhaps the best conservation project of my career, so far.

There are and have been many stewards of the Hoh River Valley, perhaps the greatest being the abundant rainfall that allows for such enormous trees and the ever-present moss that grows on just about everything. The Hoh Indians were the first to arrive in the valley, and they continue to care for the salmon fishery from their homes at the river's mouth. Courageous and driven pioneers carved farms and homes from the thick forest, and today their descendants work and nurture these riverfront homesteads. President Teddy Roosevelt set events in motion a century ago that led to the creation of Olympic National Park. Today the Park Service manages the pristine headwaters of the Hoh River Valley and gives people opportunities to hike, climb, and camp in this dramatic setting. For decades, the forest products industry has harvested the high-quality timber in the Hoh Valley, providing jobs and income to the area, and then replanted, ensuring the next harvest in what is some of the finest tree-growing land in the world. Since 1992, the Washington State Department of Natural Resources has operated its Olympic Experimental State Forest in the Hoh Valley, devising new methods of managing forests to provide funding to local schools, hospitals, and communities while also providing habitat for fish and wildlife.

Now there is a new steward in the valley, the Hoh River Trust. The conservation story of Hoh River Trust begins with opportunity. It is a story of changing forestry, willing sellers, far-reaching vision, bold risks, public-private collaborations, and new partnerships. When the state improved permitted forestry practices

Hoh River
emerging from its
sandstone canyon

statewide, timber companies in the Hoh Valley wanted to restructure their tree farms to better accommodate their practices with the new rules. Riverfront lands along the Hoh faced two likely fates: either convert to homesites or find another means to remain open space. This is where the nonprofit Western Rivers Conservancy saw a chance and boldly seized it. The Conservancy had started buying the land on loans. They came to me with an idea based on a simple concept.

Moss-laden bigleaf maples with new spring leaves

The federal and state government could provide funding to buy the land while the project partners raised dollars from nongovernment sources to manage the land. The federal government spends millions of dollars every year to buy land for conservation, and then usually pays to manage those lands indefinitely. Here was a chance to save the best salmon and steelhead stream in the lower 48 states and increase recreation opportunities for the hundreds of thousands of annual visitors to the Hoh Valley—and the government makes a one-time investment to make it happen. To me, it was an easy answer. I said, "Let's do it!"

The result is, again, the best conservation project of my career (so far). The people at the U.S. Fish and Wildlife Service and the Washington State Department of Natural Resources worked hard to help the project win grants to buy the land. These diligent folks succeeded year after year at the highly competitive national grant review process to bring the grant dollars to the State and to the Hoh. As a result, the Hoh River Trust now owns and manages nearly 5,000 acres along the Lower Hoh, and that figure is growing. The Trust and its mission have attracted the right people to do right by the land. As a newcomer to the valley, the Trust was at first an enigma to residents and greeted with some skepticism. After all, this is a place where many residents can count back just a few generations to the original settlers. Now its board of directors includes the descendant of a pioneer family, foresters, fisheries experts, educators, finance specialists, real estate professionals, and of course, river conservationists. The Trust, like the Hoh River, is alive and thriving.

As you read the fine essays collected in this book and view the great beauties of the Hoh captured masterfully on film by Keith Lazelle, I know you'll be struck by the many stories of the Hoh. Stories of nature and of people sometimes at odds, sometimes less so, and often wet from rain. The Hoh is a place that embodies the very spirit of the West: its tremendous natural heritage, its sublime beauty, its overwhelming challenges, its hard-fought struggles, and its champions. These stories remind me why I love this country, this state, and this river. I hope you enjoy *Fast Moving Water*.

Photography Foreword

by Art Wolfe

I first met Keith Lazelle on the Upper Hoh Road in the mid-1980s. It was early in his career, but I could sense Keith's profound love of nature then and there. It was in the winter and he was shooting backlit bigleaf maples, and I stopped and commented on how good the light was. It is evident that Keith has an intimate knowledge of the flora and fauna of the Northwest, and a deep appreciation for the Hoh River and its surrounds. This puts him in a position to capture the Hoh's fast-moving water in a way nobody else can. He has a strong sense of aesthetic beyond the documentary, which has evolved from his influences and his approach to photography.

Keith has told me that his path to serious photography began with a deeper understanding of the written art form of haiku poetry. One book in particular, called *A Haiku Journey*, a translation of 17th-century Japanese poet Basho, accompanied by the photography of Dennis Stock, captured his imagination. Keith feels that photography can be practiced as haiku in visual form. Despite its minimalist form, there is an unparalleled depth in haiku, and the art is to unleash an abundance of meaning and imagery by the very brevity of words. There is rich space for significance between simple, yet evocative, utterances.

For Keith, the art of photography works in a similar way. Committed to the spontaneity of 35mm, and these days entirely digital, Keith embraces brevity to evoke powerful meaning in his images. He does this through his use of light, color, composition, and gesture. For this, Keith owes inspiration to the New York photographers Ernst Haas—whose work has had a profound influence on me as well—and Jay Maisel, as well as Washington-based environmental and fine-art photographer Pat O'Hara.

How is it that a young photographer with Edo period Japanese inspiration and East Coast influences has rooted his life and his photography so firmly in the natural environs of the Pacific Northwest? As adaptable and diverse as his influences have been, Keith brings these elements together for an intimate and thought-provoking photographic exploration of the Olympic Peninsula.

Bigleaf maples backlit in winter light

Introduction

by Phil Davis, Hoh River Trust

It was late spring 2005 when my friend Bob Blais told me about this unique conservation project happening along the Hoh River. Although I'd spent limited time on the west end of Washington's Olympic Peninsula, the Hoh River and its lush rain forest had taken on almost mystical proportions in my sense of its place in our natural world.

The opportunity to become the executive director of the Hoh River Trust—a nonprofit land trust created to provide stewardship over thousands of acres of land within this awe-inspiring river valley—was humbling and intimidating, to say the least. I was intrigued mostly out of my love of rivers and the opportunity to work on something that touched my core.

As I dug deeper I quickly learned about some of the challenges I would be facing, from community ambivalence and funding obstacles to competing agendas. Since my business career had certainly prepared me to deal with these sorts of things, none of them were enough to discourage me. But it became clear that what I really needed to do was to experience the Hoh River firsthand. So I arranged a couple of trips: one a tour of the Trust's properties with Josh Kling from Western Rivers Conservancy and the other a snorkeling expedition into one of the Hoh's tributaries with Nick Demerice, James Starr, and John McMillan, all from the Wild Salmon Center. Western Rivers Conservancy had the vision to create the Hoh River Recreation and Conservation Corridor. They bought the Hoh River properties and secured the funding that allowed Hoh River Trust to acquire them. The Wild Salmon Center also helped bring funding to the project and has conducted an extensive and ongoing study of the Hoh's great salmon habitats. The land tour was inspiring, but it was my snorkeling baptism that closed the deal for me.

Sword ferns and summer river

It was one of those stunning bluebird days where you'd be hard pressed to imagine the winter wrath that awaits. Eighty degrees, sparkling sunlight, full of every shade of green imaginable, and a river calmed by an extended dry spell.

We set out mid morning to one of the Hoh's most important tributaries, where wild fish migrate to spawn and seek refuge from the harsher main-stem channel. Our mission was to don mask and snorkel and plunge into the wonderment of this underwater world. James and John, who had spent the last several years conducting snorkeling surveys over countless miles of the Hoh and its tributaries, knew just where to go.

The first step in the ceremony was changing into a rented neoprene dry suit—a procedure that I completed successfully, if not gracefully, and which included a full roadside disrobing that caused just enough nervous perspiration to make the slightly undersized neoprenes that much more difficult to squeeze into. I'm grateful that no one brought a camera that day.

After a short walk to the stream and a brief orientation on what I was to do, it was time to venture in. To be honest, my expectations were pretty low. Here we were standing on the side of this small stream, barely six feet wide, with no visual indication of anything too exciting below the surface. But it was a beautiful day, I was spending it with some very interesting people, and I was doing something I'd never done before.

As I edged myself along from the shallow tail-out into the deeper section of the pool, laid out on my stomach, I was able to fully submerge my mask. With the water level now above my ears, the sounds of our world were shut off, heightening the clarity of the view through my mask. And what a fish-eye view it was.

This innocuous pool just a couple feet deep and no larger than a basketball key sprang to life. Three-inch-long juvenile coho schooled together and swam up to my mask, splaying their white-tipped fins to make them seem larger and more intimidating to this benign stranger. Steelhead parr sensed my presence and darted out of sight as I struggled to keep track of their whereabouts. Fingerling chinook salmon held in their protected cover near the stream bank, almost as if they knew of their royal status even at their fractional size.

As I neared the head of the pool readying for my departure, I noticed a couple of shadowy figures tucked under a large rootwad overhang: two beautiful

17-plus-inch cutthroat, gorging on the bugs as they were delivered to their prime lie. I just lay there for several more minutes, taking it all in.

What a spectacular experience. To see the interplay of all these fish, with the sunlight and shadows dancing across the water's surface, undisturbed by the airy world above, was truly inspiring. Witnessing such life and complexity in a single pool in the Hoh system made me fully understand and appreciate the importance of this place that is so removed from most of our day-to-day lives. In August of that year, I took the job of executive director of the Hoh River Trust.

Fast Moving Water has been a real joy to create. The passion that people have for this river and its ecosystem is palpable. We've tried to capture that through the beautiful imagery of Keith Lazelle's inspiring photographs and with the thoughtful voices and varied perspectives of the people who tell their stories about this ecological treasure. I hope you enjoy the book, and are inspired to find your own way to recognize the special places in our natural world that are so important to our collective psyche.

Tributary pool and riffle

Ocean's Gift

by Tim McNulty, Writer, Poet

For as long as humans have lived on this rain-dampened corner of the Northwest coast, we've told stories of the places that inspire us. Among my favorites are the old Quileute and Hoh tales of *T'ist'ilal,* Thunderbird. The Thunderbird of legend lived in an ice cave beneath Blue Glacier at the headwaters of the Hoh River. He was all-powerful. Lightning bolts flashed from his eyes. His wings, wide as two war canoes, clapped thunder and darkened skies. Thunderbird hunted whales in the vast Pacific. During a particularly severe winter, he delivered one to the starving people. In some stories, Thunderbird grew angry when Quileute hunters approached his cave, thundered his wings, and hurtled ice and rocks down the mountainside.

Thunderbird is more tolerant of pilgrims today. But the weather-summoning power of his old home on Mount Olympus, the earth-grinding force of the ice it carries, and the life-giving energy of the river it sends thundering and gliding to the sea reign mightily over the Hoh Valley. To me, *T'ist'ilal* is a worthy embodiment of the wild and nurturing power of the magnificent watershed. From its glacial source, throughout its wildlife-rich valley forest, to the whales that feed by its teeming estuary, the Hoh River has shaped the character of a region. Like a mountain god who feeds the sea, it brings to life everything that lies between.

Of all the rivers that spill from the dizzying array of Olympic peaks, none issues from so grand and powerful a source or nourishes so rich and productive an ecosystem as the Hoh. No other Olympic river attracts near the number of visitors from around the world. And few rivers anywhere receive such fierce allegiance from those who know and love them. In a land of wild, free-flowing rivers, the Hoh stands apart.

Spring alders and snowy Hoh Peak

Surging nearly 60 miles from its source at Hoh Glacier to the Pacific, the river gathers the bulk of glacial runoff from the Mount Olympus ice fields. Thickened by up to 240 inches of precipitation annually and covering some 10 square miles, the Olympus glaciers contain more than half the glaciated area and three-quarters of the ice in the range. Stir in an average 140 inches of rainfall in the upper valley, and it is no surprise that the Native American name for the Hoh (*Ohalet* in Quileute) means "fast moving water." For most of the year, the river is a blue-gray welter of rain, ice melt, and glacial silt careering through an emerald valley of incomparable beauty. In summer its deep green pools invite the soul to linger. I've worked, hiked, and climbed in the Hoh Valley for more than 30 years now, slogged about in the winter mud of logging landings, and scribbled poems on high, windy ridges. But each time I enter the valley, no matter the season or weather, I'm captured by its magic.

"If there is magic on this planet," wrote anthropologist Loren Eiseley, "it is contained in water." And if a river has the power to carry all of the past and the promise of the future in its flow, it is this river.

The Hoh River is the child of ice and uplift, of colliding plates, the rasp of glaciers, and the eternal breath of Pacific winds. In all its aspects, the Hoh is a gift from the sea. For millions of years, subducting seafloors collided and scraped against the continent's edge. Mountains of riverborne sediments were bent, buckled, and plastered against the land's edge like flatcars of rock hitting a mountain wall. Forty million years of deepening sea bottom were scraped by the blade of continental shelf and piled chaotically beneath a coastal sea. As the mountain mass grew over the past 10 or 20 million years, it breached sea level and began to intercept the moisture-saturated winds from the Pacific. As moist air rose and cooled, it condensed and fell as rain. And as runoff channels sought the weakened strata along west-tending faults in the fractured rock, the ancestral Hoh was born.

It was a modest stream at first, gently folded between rounded hills, until the coming of Pleistocene ice. As glaciers massed on the high Olympics, they plucked and quarried the undulating mountains into sharpened ridges and peaks. As ice deepened on the tough sandstone heights of Mount Olympus, the Hoh, Blue, White, and Ice River glaciers merged into a valley glacier. It ground down the channel of the Hoh, straightening and carving the long, flat, U-shaped valley, leaving it floored with glacial rubble and walled with steep 3,000- to 4,000-foot ridges for much of its length.

Winter light along the river, Schmidt Bar

On several occasions throughout the two million years of the Pleistocene, glaciers scoured the Hoh Valley. Because the initial faults tended slightly southwest, following the general direction of the subducting seafloor, the Hoh and other west-side valleys are aligned with winter storm tracks. Pacific fronts deliver prodigious amounts of rain to the forested valley of the Hoh, and as mentioned, a stupendous snowpack to the dominant mountain at its head. During relatively dry summer months, coastal fog is drawn inland up the valley, where it condenses on millions of conifer needles and drips to the ground, adding precious moisture at a critical time of the year.

The wonderful combination of these elements, unfolding over millennia in the Hoh Valley, has given birth to forest, river, and wildlife communities of unsurpassed beauty and richness.

Young hairy woodpecker in cavity nest snag

The temperate rain forests of the Olympic Peninsula are renowned worldwide for their size, age, and stature, for their biological complexity, for the lush extravagance of mosses, lichens, and ferns that carpet the ground and drape the canopy, and for the amazing diversity of wildlife that thrives here.

Forests of Sitka spruce and western hemlock dominate the Pacific coast from Coos Bay, Oregon, to the Gulf of Alaska. But on the Olympic Peninsula, this coastal forest was drawn far up the glacier-carved valleys. There, protected from coastal windstorms, amply watered by near-continuous rains, and misted through the summer by rivers of coastal fog, the spruce-hemlock forest thrived. The latitude and moderate temperatures were right, and the threat of fire dampened. Record-size specimens of Sitka spruce, western hemlock, western red cedar, and Douglas fir are found here, trees that test the size limit for their species. Along with impressive broad-leaved trees of alder, cottonwood, and bigleaf maple, they form a towering, many-layered canopy of refracted green light. Vine maples twine between their trunks seeking shafts of sunlight. Clusters of sword ferns and salmonberry leaves spread across the forest floor, and a green carpet of shamrock-like oxalis, moss, and wildflowers covers the ground.

Beyond the great trees, other characteristics mark the rain forest as unique. Centuries-old "snags," standing dead trees, are scattered throughout the forest like totems. Riddled with pileated woodpecker holes, they provide dens for owls, bats, pine martens, flying squirrels, Vaux's swifts, and a grateful host of forest birds. As snags fall to the forest floor, they become homes for a menagerie of small mammals, amphibians, and insects, not to mention fungi and bacteria that play a key role in recycling nutrients.

Most conspicuous among downed logs in the Hoh forest are "nurse logs." With the forest floor too crowded with growth to provide much room for tree seedlings, damp moss in the bark crevices of fallen trees provides welcoming beds for seedlings. Nurse logs offer warmth, nutrients, moisture, and sometimes protection from grazers. Of the hundreds of seedlings that may feather a nurse log, a few manage to sink their roots into forest soils and grow into mature trees.

Where several have sprung from a single log, often long since rotted away, the resulting "colonnade" offers a poignant image of new life rising from death.

When the late naturalist and teacher Grant Sharpe was conducting research in the Hoh Rain Forest, he designed the Hall of Mosses interpretive trail at Olympic National Park's Hoh Visitor Center. The trail winds through a spectacular grove of maples whose limbs are covered with thick cushions of mosses, lichens, liverworts, and ferns and draped with hanging scarves of club moss. It is the most popular nature walk in the park. More recent research in the Hoh Valley has discovered that these aerial gardens contain more than 130 epiphytes and support twice the biomass of the forest floor. They also harbor a complex world of invertebrates: mites, springtails, and spiders, many of which were new to science. Along with the more well-known canopy dwellers such as spotted owls, marbled murrelets, flying squirrels, and redback voles, these invertebrates suggest a barely known arboreal world as rich and complex as the valley floor.

In autumn, the valley becomes the princely domain of the largest of North America's elk, the Roosevelt elk. During the fall rut, the forest echoes with whistling calls as the bulls defend their sizable harems against male challengers. Fall in the Upper Hoh is the best time to observe them. Yellow leaves are dropping from trees and shrubs, and the elk, preoccupied as they are, are much less skittish than the summer herds of the high country.

Elk have been known to occupy Olympic valleys for at least 3,000 years, and signs of their presence are everywhere. Some Hoh Valley elk remain in the lower forest year-round in small herds of 15 to 25. As they browse their home ranges, they shape the character of the valley, keeping the shrub layer in check and creating open, parklike conditions on the forest floor. By favoring some plants over others, elk even influence the nature of the forest itself. Vine maples, young hemlocks, and red cedars are favorite browse, but spruce less so. Studies in the South Fork Hoh suggest that the dominance of spruce in these forests may owe more than a passing nod to browsing elk. Researchers also found that areas browsed heavily by elk actually support a greater variety of understory plants. Hidden in the beauty of the Hoh forest is a brilliant example of a magnificent species coevolved with its habitat.

Colonnade of mature
trees along vanished
nurse log

Forest floor detail, Oregon oxalis, and lobaria lichen

In a similar way, the forest itself has shaped the character of the Hoh River and over time made possible the bounty of salmon and other native fish found here. When valley glaciers retreated, they left behind a raw, rubble-filled landscape subject to floods, washouts, and wild fluctuations in river levels. Then the climate cooled around 6,000 years ago, and forests similar to today's reclaimed the landscape. Large trees shaded streams and stabilized slopes. Overhung roots and banks furnished protective cover. When trees fell across streams, they created pools and riffles—resting and feeding places for fish. As fallen trees formed logjams, they slowed the river's flow, dissipating its erosive power and spreading sediment-rich floodwaters across broad valley bottoms. Side channels served as protected habitats for fish during high water. Fallen organic matter fed invertebrates that fed young fry. Over the centuries, the forest made the Hoh a sanctuary for wild salmon.

Today, great chinook salmon ascend the Hoh in spring and fall runs. Summer and winter steelhead spawn in the river's turbulent waters, and fall rains bring sizable runs of coho and chum. Some stocks, such as coho and winter steelhead, make their way well into the upper river, and can be seen spawning nearly 50 miles inland. Bull trout swim out to sea and ascend nearby rivers. Cutthroat trout, mountain whitefish, Pacific lamprey, and a host of other wild fish find habitat throughout the river.

Salmon are unique. They complete the circle in the downstream rush of river to sea. In the fast-moving waters of the Hoh, they alone bring nutrients from the ocean—carbon, nitrogen, phosphorous—to the inland forest. When they spawn and die, they nourish the entire watershed community, from aquatic plants and invertebrates to resident fish. Over 100 wildlife species, from black bears to dippers, are known to benefit from the salmon's journey. And their dragged-off carcasses nurture the growth of forest trees.

Like *T'ist'ilal*, who captured a whale for the people, the bright swimmers of the Hoh carry gifts from the sea back to the forest community. For millennia, humans have been part of the circle. We come to the bright, flashing waters of the Hoh for our own nourishment and renewal—and in our own ways, in our different languages, we express our wonder, our allegiance, and our thanks.

Above Hoh Valley

by Tim McNulty

In the late slant of mountain light,
    a silver ribbon follows after itself.
River music lifts
    through spruce and hemlock
        a mile below.

—

A low sea of cloud
    hems the foothills
as a finger of mist
    sifts past the first swells of mountain,
        drifts upstream.

—

Along a furrow
    in a sandstone wall,
the slightest star-shaped flower
    steals something from the southern sky.

—

Snow trickles into a still pool;
    a sheet of glass
        widens across the stars.

Mount Olympus,
avalanche lilies, and
Hoh Valley fog

Salmonberry blossom

A break in the weather at dusk

Red alder grove
in spring

Red alders against a blue winter sky

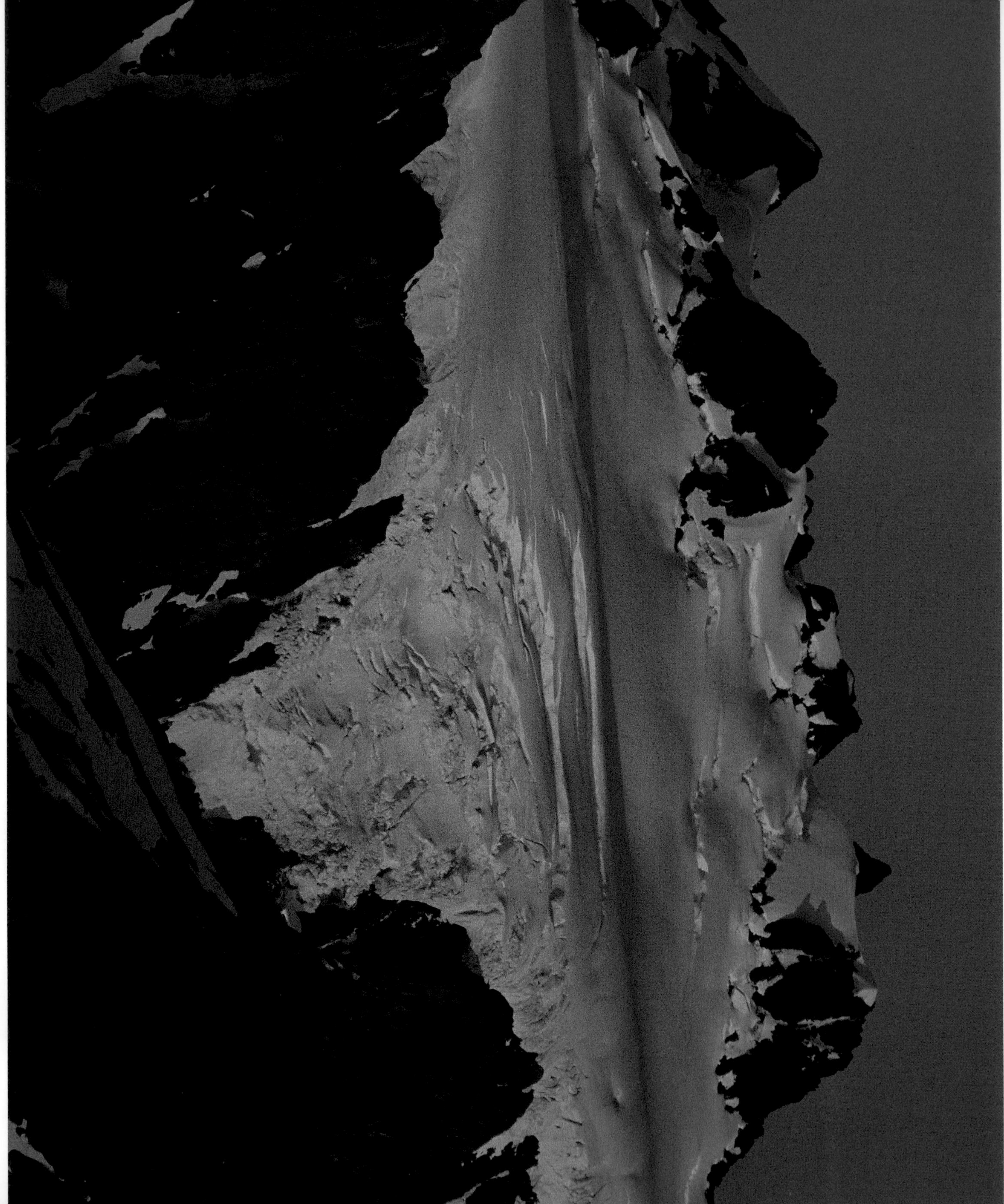

Mount Olympus

by Jack Ganster, Mountaineer

The Crown Jewel of the Olympics

The grandeur of the Olympic Mountains is evident throughout Olympic National Park, but there are no more spectacular examples than Mount Olympus and the Hoh River Valley.

The moment I saw some old photos of this remote, glacier-covered peak, I knew that I wanted to climb it. I was a backcountry skier living in Vermont at the time, and those images of year-round snow and sharp rugged peaks drew me in like a moth to a flame.

Convinced that this place was the high country of my dreams, I moved across the continent to Port Angeles. I wanted to explore the hidden reaches of this mountain landscape, to see if my dreams could be real. I was so focused on reaching this alpine playground that I did not foresee what a variety of natural worlds my journey would take me through.

I had been in town for only a month when I put together a trip for the two days I had off for the fourth-of-July holiday. My goal was to ski from as high up the mountain as I could. I had no idea how ambitious this plan was—after all, it was *only* a 42-mile round-trip hike.

I was new to the Olympics but not to hiking. I had hiked the entire Appalachian Trail in 1985, and that's where I met my Port Angeles connection, Steve Teufert. He had local experience and suggested I team up with someone to be safe, especially on the mountain. I quickly agreed and he introduced me to Robert, who was also new to town.

Arriving at the Hoh River trailhead after sunset, we set off in the approaching darkness. My anticipation of the upper reaches of the hike kept me from realizing just how amazing my surroundings were as we hiked a short three miles before making camp. I was simply happy to be on my way.

Dawn light on Snow Dome, Mount Olympus

Setting out at first light the next morning, however, I soon realized that there was more to this valley than an approach to a mountain. As the sun rose higher into the sky, we were greeted by a thousand shades of green. Trees of gigantic proportions created a mesmerizing scene.

Shafts of light descending to the valley floor invited me forward, deeper into this living cathedral. Douglas fir, western red cedar, and Sitka spruce dominated the forest. Some of the largest trees of several species are found here, including an amazing western red cedar that is more than 60 feet around at its base.

I began to think of not only the history of hiking in the Hoh Valley and the summit attempts on Mount Olympus, but also the hundreds of years that these trees had experienced. Individual cedars can grow for 1,000 years, and Douglas fir can live for 700 years!

This was my first encounter with an old-growth forest, and the joy of the discovery carried me up the valley. The flat valley miles clicked off behind me. My arrival at High Hoh Bridge, 13 miles in and a dramatic 150 feet above the river, marked the beginning of the real work of climbing the mountain.

The trail gained less than 800 feet during the first 13 miles, and the lush rain forest remained a constant companion. But that was about to change. There are several zones of vegetation that you hike through on your way to the mountain. The effect is of traveling 100 miles north for every 500 feet of elevation gained.

We passed on a quick dip into Elk Lake in an effort to get to our base camp at Glacier Meadows. I soon regretted not taking advantage of that cool water, and now I always stop for a swim before taking on the final steep 2.5 miles to camp. It was during this stretch that the elevation change really became noticeable, as we trudged through the montane zone and approached the subalpine.

I carried a heavy pack with the combined weight of ski and climbing gear, and had made the decision to leave the tent behind and sleep "under the stars." But there was little sleep under the star-filled sky that night as I filled with the anticipation of my first experience on a living glacier.

Hoh River trail and rain-forest trees

Hoh River canyon
from the
High Hoh Bridge

The sky had barely begun to lighten when I was up and ready to begin the day. The first mile was painful as my legs tried to recover from the previous day's effort. But seeing mountain goats just 200 yards away made me feel that I had entered their world. They seemed amused at my feeble pace.

Then the moment I had been waiting for arrived in stunning fashion. We topped the moraine and were rewarded with an extraordinary view. Blue Glacier lay still in the shade several hundred feet below. And glowing in the early morning sun was Snow Dome and the summit of Mount Olympus 3,000 feet above. This was what I had come for, and I suddenly knew I was in my element. I never tire of this view, and I will continue to make this trek for the glory of this moment alone.

The coolness emanating from the ice of the glacier added to the experience of what felt like a walk in a moonscape. I was naive that first trip and just flew across the broken ice, leaving Robert to chase me down. I now know that many climbers have sprained ankles and even broken legs on the lower Blue Glacier, and that it should be negotiated with care.

As we headed up the climbing route after crossing the mostly flat glacier, the terrain became steep and I was finally happy that I had carried my skis. What I didn't realize was that we were climbing the Snow Dome, which averages 300 inches deep and has been drilled as deep as 1,000.

While the average rainfall at the Hoh Ranger Station is 140 inches a year, Mount Olympus receives the equivalent of 240 inches. Because the precipitation is measured in rainfall, the upper reaches of the mountain receive as much as 100 feet of snow!

On that first climb, I imagined what it must have been like to try this ascent 50 or even 100 years earlier: to be a pioneer climber of the mountain. I had entered the world of the old photos that drew me here.

It was easy to imagine that there had never been an ascent before the one I was undertaking. The snow and ice were trackless. There was no one else on the mountain. The feeling was of being a Mount Olympus pioneer.

I have since come to realize that it is not unusual to be on a Mount Olympus summit adventure with no other climbing parties on the mountain. Although it is the third-most-glaciated peak in the continental United States (behind only Mount Rainier and Mount Baker), it is remote enough to record fewer summit parties all summer than Mount Rainier can have in a single busy weekend.

We soon realized that our time was running out and spent 20 minutes eating and cursing our two-day schedule. We decided on ascending the direct route and hoped for the best.

The steep slope was intimidating, and as we skirted around a deep crevasse, I knew I would be starting my ski run below that point. We came across another more substantial opening, and although the summit block was just within reach, our time was up and we needed to descend.

When we paused to take in the high views, all our efforts were richly rewarded. Only 35 miles to the west, the Pacific Ocean shone a sparkling gold. In every other direction, mountains and valleys spread below. The Olympics stood in stark detail, and the neighboring ranges were clearly visible in the distance. Seeing the Coastal Range in Canada to the north and the Cascades, including Mount Baker, to the east, we were more than happy with our destination. Even though we hadn't reached the rocky summit, we felt fulfilled.

As this satisfaction set in, I realized this was only the halfway point. Now I would get to ski down the 3,000 feet that I had just climbed, excluding the huge gap that I needed to down-climb around. Putting my skis on while clinging to a 50-degree slope proved spooky, but once this was accomplished, the pitch eased and seemed merely challenging.

I wasn't sure that skiing would be easier than glissading, especially when Robert sat down and slid down the hill. My legs burned from the effort of the approach and the effect of skiing 12 inches of slush. But the pain took a backseat to the joy of carving turns down the Snow Dome, and the effortless glide across the Blue proved a delight while Robert had to renegotiate the icy terrain on foot.

I was sorry to leave this mountainous world, but we had to keep moving. Back in the valley, I once again found myself in the most incredibly lush surroundings. It all seemed surreal, and my recurring thought was "How could all of this be in one place?"

At the time I thought, "What a special place." After 16 years and several summit visits, I now know how absolutely special this place is. For the incredible forest and spectacular peak at the upper end, the Hoh River and Mount Olympus are without peer.

Blue Glacier in late summer, Mount Olympus

Love at First Listen

by Gordon Hempton, Natural Sound Recordist

Everyone should be blessed with a place they can call their own—a place where they can feel intimately connected with the rest of life; a place where they can shed, like water off a salal leaf, the cares (most of them trivial, after all) of a busier, stressful, noisy life back home; a place of contemplation and reinvigoration and peace. For me, that place is the Hoh Valley. I discovered it with my ears.

But not initially. I first walked up the Hoh Valley trail alone the summer before my senior year as a botany major at the University of Wisconsin. This was 1975, and I was taking a summer exchange course on photography at Evergreen State College. I backpacked in with an Olympus OM-2 and plenty of Kodachrome 25, intent on photographing what I'd been told was a spectacular, towering temperate rain forest. I took plenty of photos, all right, but looking at them later, I felt frustrated, and didn't really know why until some six years later, when I returned to the Hoh not as a sightseer, but as a listener, and began to appreciate the rare charm of this secluded valley. This came early in my career as a nature sound recording artist and acoustic ecologist.

Since then, I've circled the globe three times searching for the pristine sounds of nature untrammeled by the noise of man on every continent but Antarctica. I've set up my equipment in every state in the nation and in most of America's national parks. Sadly, I'm almost always disappointed. Typically, there's truck traffic from a highway 10 miles away. Or the steady, low-frequency hum of a paper mill. Or noise intrusions from overhead aircraft. More and more I find myself listening for something that has vanished, which explains why I keep coming back to the Hoh. Tucked away in a remote, often overlooked corner of the continental United States, in a rare national park unbisected by a roadway, beneath few prescribed jetliner routes, the Hoh Valley remains a listener's paradise and a national treasure. I believe it's the quietest spot in the lower 48.

Grasses after summer rain

Even in the rainy season, the listening is good. Every kind of rain can be heard, and every leaf and forest fiber seems to produce its own sound if you can get close enough to hear it: the pattering of the rain on top of a dried fallen maple leaf . . . the soft tap of a lone raindrop onto moss. There's a fascinating delay factor in this Pacific rain forest, a terrestrial take on starlight. Because of the towering, many-layered structure of the Hoh forest, you rarely hear rain falling straight from the sky. What you're actually hearing is forest showers, drizzles, and drops, secondary precipitation that may take a Rube Goldberg path through the forest canopy, off a succession of different leaves, and then, finally, to the ground.

Fall is my favorite time of year in the Hoh. When I arrive at the Visitor Center parking lot and turn off the engine, the first sound I hear is the tinkling of the motor as it begins to cool. I can be nearly a mile up the trail and still hear the *beep-beep* of somebody's remote door lock shouting out that the job is done. But step by step up the gentle trail, the ties to civilization fall away. Climbing up the old riverbank, onto the first plateau, home to some of the Hoh's largest trees, I'm reminded of a cathedral. The size and spacing of the giant spruces are nature's counterpart to the columns of the National Cathedral in Washington, D.C. And there's a soul-satisfying, cathedral-like quiet here because the river is distant at this point on the hike. In the absence of wind and rain, my sound meter has registered in the low-20-decibel range, as quiet as a bedroom at night.

Here, you'll hear the far-off hoot of owls, even during the daytime. And the sledge-hammer blows of the pileated woodpecker. And the high-pitched twittering cascade of the winter wren, a great favorite of mine. You'll hear them much more often than you'll see them, which is why even the best photographs can't capture the full experience of the Hoh. Sound does not hide behind a fallen tree or a bend in the trail. Our ears take us where our eyes cannot—and in a listening sanctuary like the Hoh, reward us again and again.

Farther up the trail, you come to a grove of moss-draped bigleaf maple trees that put on a spectacular show on a sunny autumn day when they're in full color and a gentle breeze begins to blow. This performance starts on high, with as few as

Ancient western
red cedars

a handful of wind-blown leaves fluttering from the upper branches, colliding with other leaves. Soft. Individual handclaps. Then a strong gust will dispatch hundreds of leaves, triggering a gentle, building applause.

A bit farther on, where the Hoh River comes into view, you may begin to smell the sweet muskiness of the elk and perhaps be fortunate enough to hear them bugle. Fall is the peak of their rutting season, and the males are announcing their challenges to other males. From a distance, echoing up and down the valley, you'll hear a high, flutish whistling sound. But up close, as here, where the elk like to come, their bugle sounds very different: throaty, aggressive, testosterone driven, and fear inspiring. Standing totally quiet and motionless, I've had elk pass within 10 feet of me, though I don't recommend such close encounters, as these are large, dangerous animals.

Another sound I've come to enjoy resonates as you step across the occasional boardwalks over wet terrain and various streams flowing into the Hoh. The native

Salmonberry and the mushroom-like lichen agaric

cedar slats replay your footsteps rather like outdoor xylophones. Yes, they announce your presence in the woods, but as they do so, you hear your footfalls, and as you hike farther and farther up the Hoh trail from the asphalt parking lot, you can hear your rhythm slow in tune with your sense of urgency.

About three miles from the Visitor Center begins the rare opportunity for true aural solitude. You've passed out of earshot of activities at the camping area at the trailhead and the turnaround point for many day hikers. It's not uncommon to walk for hours and pass only one or two hikers, generally descending from the mountains after a several-day backcountry experience. They no longer smell like their laundry detergent. Nor are they fretting about things left undone back at home or at work. I love the contented looks on their faces.

At 3.2 miles up the trail, I turn left off the path when I reach a cavelike opening made by a cojoined stilted spruce and hemlock, and soon step through a low muddy area often crisscrossed with elk tracks. I stop when I come to a small red rock atop a chest-high moss-covered log. The stone, given to me years ago by David Forlines, the late cultural elder of the Quileute Tribe, marks the spot that I've designated One Square Inch for Quiet—a sanctuary of silence that I am defending from all human noise intrusions. My actions to defend this single square inch, I believe, may protect as much as 1,000 square miles (visit www.onesquareinch.org for more information).

We need quiet places like this to bring us closer in touch with our planet—and also ourselves. Living in suburbia and the city, as I once did myself, we've come to equate the loudest sounds with the most important. (TV watching and movie viewing only reinforce this.) We listen to the loudest first. The squeaky wheel gets our attentive grease. But in a profoundly quiet place like the Hoh Valley, you come to learn that there is a wealth of meaning and understanding carried on the musical score of delicate and subtle sounds—natural notes that can be enjoyed only in the absence of man-made noise and only after quieting yourself emotionally as well.

Listen long and hard, and you'll not only hear pine wind but also learn to discern what species of evergreen you're listening to. Spruce wind . . . cedar wind . . . longleaf pine . . . shortleaf pine—the shorter the needle, the higher the pitch; the longer the needle, the lower the pitch. In the Hoh, a dedicated listener can be led blindfolded to a spot and identify the surrounding trees by the music they make. And discern the future in the forest's most delicate rain of all: the soft taps of mature seeds, landing first on the firm, hard salal leaves before sliding to rest on the fecund forest floor.

Another sound that I love is birthed in the Hoh but not heard there. I've spent hours listening to it on the pebbled shore of nearby Rialto Beach. Winter's storms and floods often pull riverbank-dwelling Sitka spruces into the torrent and carry them down the Hoh into the Pacific. Some wash up on shore, frequently bearing enormous cavelike root cavities big enough to walk into. Giant ears of wood, I call them, for I've spent hours and hours enthralled by the unforgettable listening experience they afford. This, after all, is the same wood used to make violins and the sounding board of Steinway pianos. Step inside one of these ears of wood and you'll hear a secret symphony born in the Hoh, music that unfolds as the huge rolling waves sweep up through the soft sand, then into the tinkly pea gravel, then farther up the beach, rattling the ever larger, surf-sifted and -smoothed stones—and then recede. With the seasonal changes in the waves, the beach sings a different song in the winter than it does in the summer.

I'm convinced I would have never heard that distinctive music had I not, decades ago, put away my camera (for a time) and hiked into the Hoh Valley carrying sound-recording equipment instead. Ever since, the Hoh has taught me much. Its sonic wonders have helped me hone my listening skills and opened my senses to unheard opportunities around the world. Simply stated, the Hoh has won my heart—not at first sight, but at first listen . . . and 100th listen—for it is surely one of the last truly quiet places on Earth, one of the planet's most sublime natural symphony halls.

Gordon Hempton, aka The Sound Tracker®, is at work on a book about quiet and noise for Simon & Schuster's Free Press that prominently features One Square Inch for Quiet in the Hoh Valley.

Middle Rock with
seagulls and pelicans,
Hob River mouth

Taft Creek in autumn

Looking up the mossy trunk of an ancient Sitka spruce

On Bell's Terms

by Jon Preston, Park Ranger, Hoh Ranger Station

I had been warned about a particular cow elk weeks before I set out to photograph the resident herd of 30 or so as they passed through the famous Hall of Mosses. It was a great opportunity to capture images with the perfect trademark backdrop of the Hoh Rain Forest. Photography, when it comes to wildlife, is part luck with a heaping portion of preparation and patience. In anticipation of their projected course, I positioned myself well ahead of the herd and sat down on the ground and waited for them to browse their way to my position.

Elk are widespread throughout the West, but here in the lush windward foothills of Olympic National Park they exhibit some unique characteristics that set them apart from their counterparts elsewhere. And because of the lack of human predation since the creation of this refuge in 1938, the region within the boundaries of the park is usually running close to the ecosystem's carrying capacity. The elk population is estimated at more than 4,000 animals. They have been a source of interest since they were nearly eliminated by hunting in the late 19th and early 20th centuries. This wholesale slaughter was the catalyst for Theodore Roosevelt to create Mount Olympus National Monument in 1909, thus forming the core of what was later to become Olympic National Park.

They have been called many names, but these particular animals that occupy the old-growth spruce and hemlock forests on the Pacific slope are considered a subspecies by some taxonomists: *Cervus elaphus roosevelti,* or more commonly Roosevelt elk. The herd of elk I was stalking this fine spring day had been the subject of a recent study by park biologists that reinforced the belief that these elk had home ranges. This was in contrast to their easterly brethren, who migrate upslope in the summer and back to low-elevation pastures in the winter. So at any given moment at any time of the year, if I was near the Visitor Center at the end of the Hoh Road, I was always within a mile of this herd. To the biologists this

Elk in Hall of Mosses

herd was known as Kernel 01, which is the point at which I will deviate from the scientific perspective. I called them the campground herd.

Working as the ranger in charge of resource education put me in the position of go-to person for the visiting public for information about the Hoh Valley. I have spent a fair amount of time in the valley and have used the opportunity to try and include myself within the ebb and flow of life there. From the day I started the job, there were always the elk. On any given day they were in the campground, in the parking lot, on the drain field, along the road, or on the gravel bar across the river. You just had to spend some time and be observant. It did not take long for me to notice something out of the ordinary about one of the cows. She wore a rather bulky canvas-covered collar with an even bulkier box attached to it, hanging loosely beneath her chin. This was the transmitter that provided home-range information to the interested scientists. The battery had run out years before, and it now hung there impotent and out of place. It was explained to me that the collar was supposed to have automatically detached itself, but a malfunction had prevented this from happening.

We who work at the Hoh Rain Forest found ourselves explaining the malfunction story to curious visitors numerous times a week. The biologists, however, rather than try to recapture the animal just to remove a collar that wasn't causing the cow any problems, left the collar alone. At some point we took to calling her Bell. I really do not remember who started this. I guess it looked like a cowbell to someone and the name stuck.

We continued to answer visitors' questions about the collar. You could anticipate the question after a while. My personal feeling, though, was that if an elk had wanted to "accessorize," she would not have picked anything close to what she was wearing—a fact that was accentuated by her temperament.

Bell was the matriarch of the campground herd. If you came across her, the other animals were close behind. Every spring, like clockwork, she would give birth to a calf. This was both a curse and a blessing. She was not in any way timid about defending the perimeter around her newborns, which could cause quite a bit of excitement around the Visitor Center now and then.

"Shooting" elk, Olympic National Park

So there I sat with my back resting against a fallen log, waiting to get my pictures. The herd was being very cooperative and moving into perfect position when from behind me I heard the crashing of brush; looking over my shoulder, I saw Bell coming toward me, her ears lowered menacingly. I was doomed and she was on me instantly. All I could think of was to shoot a picture to document my demise. Figuring I was about to be stomped into dust if I made the wrong move, I assumed a meek posture, sliding lower to the ground. To my surprise she just stood there, towering over me, looking down at me. And then, even more surprising, she lowered her head until her nose was less than an inch from my cheek and . . . sniffed! Not once but several times. I was paralyzed. She then lifted her head and vocalized the trademark elk squeak call as she took a few steps away, seeming to be careful not to step on me. There was more rustling in the salmonberry thicket behind me and out came her two yearling twin calves, born the year before. Instead of moving off, they all proceeded to graze around me—even between my feet.

Cow elk feeding near
Taft Creek

Eventually they began to move off and I was able to regain my composure, although the residual adrenaline in my blood prevented me from getting a steady shot with the camera. And so began a relationship that would continue for the next few years.

Around Memorial Day that year, as expected, she gave birth to a single calf in the campground. In an effort to give her the space she needed, we closed that loop of the campground, which allowed her to nurse the calf at a safe distance from an inquisitive public. But that was only a temporary solution because as soon as the calf got its legs, the entourage started its wandering. Maintaining a mobile perimeter was labor intensive and so we took to what the Park Service is really good at: putting up signs. For the most part, visitors behaved themselves, and as a result, so did Bell.

Visitation by this time was climbing to summertime levels, so that at any given moment during the day we had close to 1,000 visitors taking in the magnificent scenery. I had been with the Park Service long enough to know that with that many people in the area, there was always going to be one who would get too close.

Shouts from the parking lot sent me running out of the Visitor Center to find Bell cornering a visitor behind one of the bearproof trash cans. The look of terror on his face was priceless. Bell's path of pursuit could be gleaned from the camera parts littering the parking lot. As soon as I got out there, Bell sauntered off back to her calf, hidden somewhere in the tall grass of the campground.

There are always people who think their "connection" to animals can be sensed. This summer, the campground host volunteers considered themselves immune to confrontation because they were vegetarians and the elk could somehow sense this. That risky hypothesis was put to rest when one host found himself playing an extreme version of peek-a-boo with Bell around one of the campground bulletin boards for a full five minutes. She wanted to stomp him pretty bad.
They left shortly after that.

I came in to work one morning to find out that one of my seasonal employees had been walking her dog in the campground, being careful to look out for Bell before she began. Bell just plain hated dogs, probably because of some negative interaction in her history. She went out of her way to chase and corral the dog and human, stomping my coworker in the shoulder and kicking her dog before calmly walking away. Fortunately, the injury was superficial; the employee had raised horses her whole life and had been through much worse. Bell was amazing in her ability to make a point.

The wildlife biologists suggested I begin hazing her by throwing rocks and otherwise making things uncomfortable for her. I just could not bring myself to do it. I was confident that she wasn't out to do serious harm to anyone, and she really cut families with kids a lot of slack. All the while, she exhibited every characteristic of a great mother. So I spent as much time as I could making sure that visitors were kept aware, and we got through the summers with some good stories and no calls to the hospital.

The seasons came and went, and Bell continued to stay around. One late spring day, she showed up outside the Visitor Center and just stood there looking through the big glass windows at me behind the information desk. So I went outside, coming up behind her, and she began to walk up the trail. When I stopped, she stopped and looked back at me. When I began to approach, she continued onto the Spruce Nature Trail. She took a turn to the right and into a little clearing, where she soon gave birth to her new calf. That summer passed without much in the way of mishaps, and I watched the calf grow into a healthy young daughter.

The following winter, Bell vanished for the longest time. I was shocked when I finally caught sight of her early that spring. She was emaciated and her coat was dull. There wasn't anything we could do for her. Finally, she curled up next to a table in the picnic area and lay down a final time. The maintenance foreman sat next to her for a while, talked to her, and scratched between her ears. Her eyes closed. And we all grieved. She was a good mom, and I was privileged to have her as a friend.

Family of Roosevelt elk resting

phone

At Home in the Rain Forest

by Susan L. Tinney, Artist, Musician

I was 10 years old when my family moved to the Hoh Rain Forest Ranger Station, in December 1971, to be one of the first two families to live there year-round. My dad had been working for Olympic National Park for about a year, stationed at Kalaloch and Lake Quinault, but had no idea what to expect at the Hoh.

Daddy led the way in the park truck, followed by a semi pulling our mobile home. Mom, my three brothers, and I followed in the car, threading our winding way up the valley. We had been told days before our move to the Hoh that a stream had washed out one of the bridges on the one road down the valley. A makeshift bridge had been fashioned from two pieces of steel guardrail wedged between the banks of the stream. To cross, you had to line up your tires in the trough of each rail and balance your way across the creek. It felt a bit like tightrope walking in a car—and was very tricky for a semi pulling a full-sized mobile home. We arrived as they were easing the trailer to the makeshift bridge and began crossing. Mom pulled into the gravel and we stood on the wet rocks under the huge dripping trees beside the creek, hardly daring to breathe as we watched everything we owned in the world inch across on those rails. Finally, the crossing safely over, we cheered and laughed until we heard a loud scraping crunch. The edge of the bank on the far side was too sharp for such a long trailer, and it had high-centered on the rocky soil of the road's edge. The driver got out and examined our house. The frame was dented but not broken, he said, and still sound. We cheered again, a bit shakily, jumped into the car, and held our breath again as Mom maneuvered the car across and continued on our way.

That first drive through the forest to the ranger station seemed endless to me, winding through deeper and deeper woods, beside misty meadows full of trees with moss hanging impossibly long from each branch. Finally, we came to a long hill that dropped down to a beaver pond where elk were wading through the water and mist, raising their dripping heads to watch us drive slowly by, munching placidly

Phone at road's end, Hoh Visitor Center

on water plants . . . and we were at our new home. We pulled into the residential area, marveling at the size of the trees right next to where we'd live. On the next few drives up the Hoh road, we kids counted the curves in the road and nicknamed that last long hill over the beaver pond Favorite Hill because it meant we were home.

The week after we moved in, it snowed. The snow, resting lightly on the green trees, seemed to be a gesture of welcome to me. I remember thinking that we were moving to our very own Land of Oz; I couldn't imagine a place looking more magical. As it turned out, we were indeed moving to the most wonderful place I could imagine living as a kid in the 1970s—a world where it was safe for a little girl to wander alone, filled with perfect hollow-tree forts, mossy glades of giant clover, new and interesting plants, fishes, and animals as well as people who could answer just about all of our endless questions about them, and where nobody cared if I didn't own designer jeans. That winter I felt like an explorer charting new ground. I discovered that stands of bracken ferns would weave together and hold several inches of snow about two feet off the ground, and if I tunneled very carefully in, I could lie beneath the snow on dry ground, in a little forest of slightly hairy stems. When I rolled onto my back, my roof was a black tracery of the lacy ferns, the snow between luminous with the daylight outside my silent, mossy world.

One of the families living with us those two years was that of Bud Hanify, an "old school" ranger who as a young man had helped to build many of the original trails into the park, carrying lumber and woodstoves for the shelters by horse and mule in the 1930s. He had built and repaired trails, traveling by foot, horse, mule, and helicopter. Bud was a wonderful storyteller, and I'll never forget sitting in the Hanifys' living room on winter evenings, sweet pipe smoke curling around Bud's head as he told us about forging trails through the wilderness of the new park. He truly loved the place, and his stories of run-ins with bears and mountain lions, living isolated miles up-trail for months while they built the Olympus Guard Station, fired my imagination and inspired me to explore the place. Of his stories, one of my favorites was about Orson Wells's broadcast of *The War of the Worlds*, on Halloween Eve of 1938. Bud had been up-trail, and came back to a cabin he was sharing that fall with another ranger. Shouting through the locked door, he

South Fork Hoh River

in winter

discovered that his friend had barricaded himself in the cabin with his radio and a shotgun. To get his bath, Bud had to convince his friend that he wasn't a Martian come to kill him with laser beams. So he sat down outside the cabin door and talked, until his friend finally believed it was him.

We attended school 30 miles from the ranger station at Forks, the nearest town. Our daily trip started with a car ride to our closest neighbors, the Lewis Ranch, seven miles away and just outside the park border. Marilyn Lewis would drive us to the highway in a small bus, picking up the kids who lived in the Lower Hoh area on the way, then we'd catch the regular school bus for the remainder of the trip. It took us well over two hours, twice a day, and the trips were rarely dull. Several times we were the first to discover that a creek had washed the road out; if it was close enough to the Lewis Ranch, we'd walk the rest of the way, and otherwise we'd drive back home. Mom was determined to get us to school; often, if a washout or a tree across the road was something that could be handled in an

Woodland mushroom

hour or so, she'd drive us all the way to Forks once the road was clear. Almost daily we would stop to let a herd or two of elk cross the road, counting out the cows and bulls for the naturalist's charts. The first spring, a huge bird's nest was built on a snag across the river; we identified the builders as ospreys, and craned our necks and shared the binoculars every time we drove by to catch glimpses of the magnificent birds, and later the babies.

My brother Dave and I, the youngest and a year apart, were odd-men-out among the kids of the families that lived at the Hoh during those two years. Too young to be interesting company for the teenagers and much older than the young children who came with the summer naturalists, we spent our time exploring on our own, creating imaginary civilizations and charting the great wilderness that was our backyard. Fascinated by the naturalist's long lists of edible plants, we tried as many as we could find. Our favorites were licorice root, oxalis, and fiddleheads. We became masters of berry-finding. Most summer days we spent on expeditions picking little wild blackberries, salmonberries, red, evergreen, or blue huckleberries, salal, blackcaps, or thimbleberries. We tried a number of the more improbably edible plants, like skunk cabbage, which must be boiled several times in fresh water, but still tastes terrible. We tried mushrooms for the first time, gathering delicate angel wings and chicken of the woods, which was both our favorite and easiest to identify.

In the 1970s, much of our current information about temperate rain forests was still being gathered, and many assumptions about the behavior of elk and other animals in this unique environment were being disproved. My brothers and I carried bird and animal checklists, and learned to recognize grouse, woodpeckers, mule deer and black-tailed deer, and rubber boa snakes. We counted the elk when we spotted herds and noted where we'd seen them, and let the rangers know when black bears or mountain lions were in the area. We learned how to tell salmon fingerlings from steelhead, how to identify trees and shrubs and ferns. We helped summer volunteers create an elk-proof enclosure in a fairly clear area in a stand of bigleaf maple, to find out how much effect the elk and deer have on the ground-cover. That spring the enclosed area was a dense column of bushes, topping and hanging over the 12-foot fence, twigs nipped right to the wire fence. It turns out that the elk and deer are the only reason there are any clear areas away from the river bottoms at the Hoh.

Being normal kids, we did occasionally break the rules. Taft Creek, which runs icy cold and crystal clear across the nature trails, had become something of a "wishing pond"; at one of the little bridges near the Visitor Center, tourists would toss in coins, as at a fountain. The money shining under that clear water was just too tempting for us; when there weren't any tourists around, we'd wade into the icy hip-deep water and scoop out what change we could before we got too cold to continue. We were eventually caught in the act and had to stop, as the rangers didn't want us to dig up the creek bottom and disturb the plants that grew there, sheltering fingerling fish and creating a safe spot for small water creatures such as muskrats and water ouzels, which visitors would occasionally spot there. We argued that the coins being tossed in were already disrupting the natural habitat, but unfortunately, their response was to mount their own expedition into the creek and carefully remove any visible coins so that people would stop tossing them in. We later found out that the money went to buy coffee for the ranger station, much to our disgust.

In the summers, my two older brothers, Don and Jim, spent as much free time as possible backpacking up the valley, over the High Divide, and back; it seemed they were always either up-trail or planning their next trip. Dave and I weren't allowed to go without adults along until years later, so we took regular day-hikes to the Happy Four shelter, 5.3 miles up the trail, with packed lunches. Dave and I finally got to take a serious overnight hike, up to the High Divide with Mom and Daddy. We were elated when we reached the Divide and set our tents out with a view across the Hoh Valley to Mount Olympus. A light mist created a spectacular rainbow that stretched from the Hoh Valley over the High Divide and down into the Seven Lakes Basin and later turned the mountain pink with the sunset. We didn't realize, though, that that pink sunset indicated a coming rain—David and I woke to find that our tent was in the path of the mountain runoff and our tent floor was four inches of running water! After finding our driest clothes, wringing out our now incredibly heavy cotton sleeping bags, and huddling around our little stove for quick mugs of chocolate and oatmeal, we started trudging the long, steep seven miles back to Olympus Guard Station, in a thick, drizzling fog. We stopped only once on the way down, when a bull elk stepped out onto a spur of rock about 15 feet from us, silhouetted perfectly black against the blanket of gray fog that filled the valley. The image took our breath away; my dad had used up all his film the night before, between the rainbow and the sunset, but I can still see that bull elk clearly, holding his great rack of antlers up, tipping his head back to bugle into the fog, almost near enough to touch. That night we slept in paper "emergency" sleeping bags at the Guard Station, occasionally woken by the rustling of the mice chewing on the bags.

Almost exactly two years after we arrived, Daddy was stationed at Kalaloch Beach, just 20 miles away on the coast. I was heartbroken that we had to leave; I had come to love the trees, the smell of the forest, the people who lived and worked there. Eventually I did adjust to living at the beach, and later to living in towns and cities, but my heart still lives at the Hoh. When I hear the words *camping, hiking, wildlife, forest,* or *home,* I smell and taste the rain forest, and see in my mind's eye that indefinable quality of light that you get only on a high overcast day, filtered through a thousand leaves.

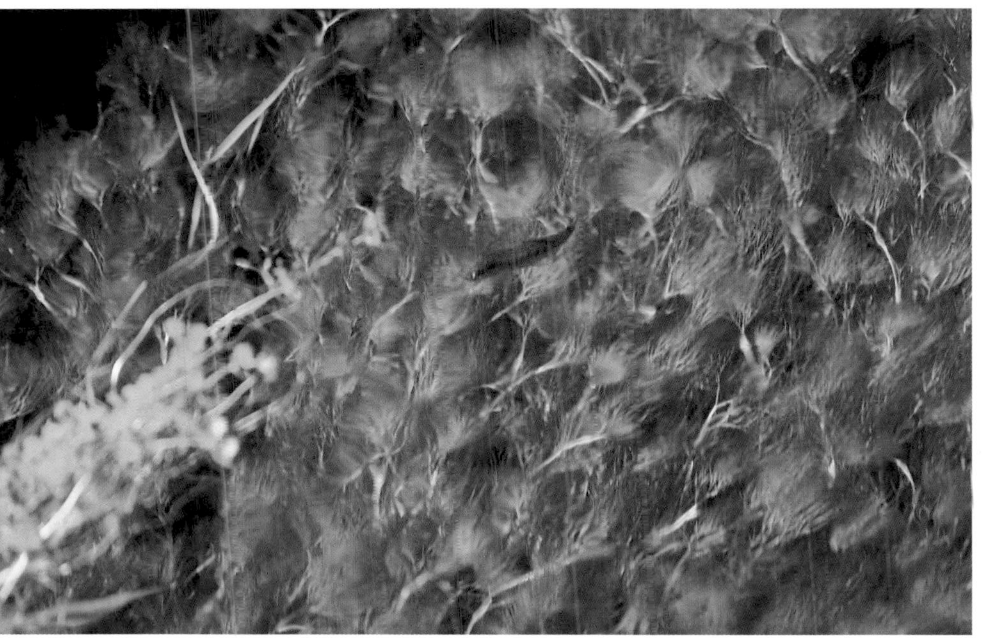

Coho fry in Taft Creek

Autumn vine maple,
Taft Creek pond

Forest wetland with western bog-laurel

Organized Chaos

by David R. Montgomery, Writer, University of Washington Professor

Speak to the earth, and it shall teach thee. — Job 12:8

I had lived in the state for all of a week and here I was, leading my first two graduate students along in the dark, hand on shoulder in front, the three of us struggling to keep to the trail and avoid running into the giant trees that dominated the floodplain. We came to the Hoh River to walk the ridges and streams of a landscape unaltered by human agencies, to get a feel for the land in the heart of the Olympic Peninsula.

And did we ever get more perspective than we bargained for. It took us hours longer than planned to descend the valley wall on the way down the ridge to the west of Mount Tom Creek and to our ford back across the river. One giant tree after another lay jackstrawed across the slope, forcing us to use the trunks of the fallen giants as elevated causeways on which to navigate downhill, something much easier than trying to climb up and over one 10- to 15-foot-diameter log after another. So we kept scampering like squirrels along each massive trunk to where we could jump over to another and continue on down the slope. Eventually, we made it back across the river at sundown and stumbled back to camp in the dark, feeling our way along the trail, weary and bedraggled.

The Hoh River is many things to many people, but to my graduate students and me the river proved quite a teacher, a natural laboratory full of surprises and insights about what rivers of the Pacific Northwest were like before they were cleared of wood and logjams to open the region for navigation and commerce. Over the 15 years since we first naively ventured up the river, the Hoh and neighboring Queets have yielded insights into floodplain ecology and geomorphology that have provided a new understanding of how the region's giant trees structured the rivers and streams of the Pacific Northwest. The story that emerged is one

Mount Olympus and Mount Tom from Hoh Lake basin

not yet in textbooks, but central nonetheless to both understanding the human footprint on the Pacific Northwest and planning for long-term stewardship of the region's fish and wildlife that depend on riverine habitats.

One of the lessons of the Hoh and Queets is that the groves of colossal ancient trees on the floodplain grow in the lee of giant logjams founded on huge logs that anchor the remains of previous generations of large trees. Perhaps this should not be surprising given that the river sweeps back and forth across its floodplain over decades or centuries, but the big trees can live for more than 500 years. For if the valley floor forest was taken out each time the river moved across the valley bottom, the oldest growth wouldn't get much more than a few hundred years old. Yet there are patches of ancient giants dotted across the floodplain. How can we explain these colonies of old growth attaining maturity on a dynamic, disturbance-prone floodplain?

When one of these leviathans falls into the river, it can ground out and dig itself in if its massive rootwad snags the riverbed like an anchor, pivoting the tree so that a wall of roots faces upstream like an arboreal catcher's mitt poised to snare other logs floating downstream. And do these anchored giants ever catch stuff. Some will eventually accumulate hundreds or even thousands of logs in a single jam intricately woven into complex structures as smaller logs floating downstream pile up on the massive obstruction. Once a stable logjam begins to grow, it can deflect the river, providing a protected area where sediment can accumulate and bury the jam-initiating logs in the floodplain. There the giant logs stay wet and can last for centuries, providing the foundation for an erosion-resistant island of stable habitat protected behind a logjam revetment. Radiocarbon dating of logjams exposed in the banks of the Queets River shows that some can remain stable for more than 1,200 years. But the jams not only catch other logs; they also slow the river flow enough to create local depositional zones where gravel and sand build up behind the jams, creating a patchwork floodplain as the individual scraps of topography piled up behind these stable jams coalesce to form the valley bottom.

"Organized chaos" is how Tim Abbe describes the logjams of the Olympic Peninsula. He should know; for his Ph.D. research at the University of Washington

Downed tree and rootwad in river

Engineered logjams,
lower river

he spent several years tramping up and canoeing down rivers in Olympic National Park, studying the ways that logjams form, how long they persist, and what influence they have on the river. Over the course of his studies he discovered that not only do logjams have systematic structure themselves, but they indirectly structure the floodplain as well by providing stable refugia where trees mature into the old growth capable of providing logs large enough to anchor future generations of logjams.

The Hoh River was one of the first places where Abbe's insights into the mechanics of logjam stability were used to guide the design of engineered logjams for erosion-control projects. Basing his work on the natural architecture of stable logjams, Abbe designed engineered versions of certain jam types that he thought could prove useful to prevent riverbank erosion and protect houses, highways, or other human infrastructure. Now such artificial logjams are being built across the state as an environmentally friendly alternative to more traditional methods of river engineering. I never imagined as we trudged back to our camp in the dark on my first day in the Hoh Valley that years later, the state Department of Transportation would be installing engineered logjams to protect the road into the Hoh River trailhead. But that's the beauty of research: you never know where it's going to lead you—just like a professor without a flashlight stumbling through the forest in the dark with a couple of graduate students in tow.

Still, just a single visit tells you that the Hoh River is much more than a laboratory. It is a symbol of both the region's natural heritage as the last domain of the giant trees that once covered the region and the working forests that surround Olympic National Park. It is a neighbor and a home to communities of people, animals, and plants. And above all, it is a wild river untamed by dams, free to wander across its floodplain and define a corridor through which the sandstone of the Olympic Mountains will eventually be returned to the sea. Yet to me, still working to better understand the rivers of the Pacific Northwest, the Hoh is foremost a teacher that offers perspectives on how to see the order in chaos and how hidden connections can structure our world.

Thunderbird's Rule

by Gary Peterson and Glynda Peterson Schaad,
Pioneer Family Descendants

In the long ago when Thunderbird ruled a world of ice, snow, and rock in the high Olympics and the sounds of his rage at trespassers rumbled down the Hoh Valley, when at fish camps far up both forks of the Hoh, drying racks overflowed with the abundance of the river and the bounty of alpine meadows, it was in those days long ago that a "house that floats on water" came to ruin at the Hole-in-the-Wall north of La Push.

Seven days later, November 1, 1808, the wet, exhausted, hungry survivors of the Russian brig *Sv. Nikolai* stumbled into the Hoh Valley on the run from Quileute warriors and headed for the safety of their sister ship, the *Kodiak*, soon to be anchored in Grays Harbor. It was not to be. On November 8, a confederation of 200 Hoh, Quileute, and Quinault Natives engaged the castaways and by clever intrigue abducted the captain's wife, Anna Petrovna, two Aleut women, and a Russian sailor.

The remaining crew and passengers escaped upriver 13 miles, where they built a fort and sustained themselves on fish from neighboring Native camps. On occasion Anna was brought upstream in attempts to exchange her for rifles, terms to which the captain agreed but the crew vetoed. Discipline in the Russian group collapsed in the second week of February 1809, when in the midst of negotiations, Anna announced her "satisfaction with the present situation and a firm refusal to join her comrades." Within 24 hours the inevitable occurred, and all Russians and Aleuts were captured. By spring all were living as slaves in coastal villages from Neah Bay to the Columbia River. On May 6, 1810, more than 18 months after the wreck of the *Nikolai*, the American ship *Lydia*, under the command of shipmaster T. Brown, dropped anchor in Neah Bay.

Cloud formations over the river

After much parley and the eventual seizure of a member of Makah royalty to speed negotiations, Captain Brown purchased 13 castaways (seven of the original crew had died in captivity). Each person cost five blankets, 35 feet of woolen cloth, a file, two steel knives, one mirror, five packets of gunpowder, and five packets of small shot. One Russian had been sold to a distant tribe and remained with them, and one was recovered by Captain George Eayres of the American ship *Mercury* on the Columbia River.

So it was that the first white woman to come to the Hoh River Valley and indeed the entire Northwest was Anna Petrovna, wife of the captain of the ill-fated *Sv. Nikolai.*

It was 40 years before white men again walked the trails of the west side of the Olympic Peninsula. According to Native legend, a canoeload of Hudson's Bay traders came by way of Pysht in about 1850 and fanned out to the south and west. A store of furs was collected at La Push and later taken by ship to Victoria. More traders and trappers followed, but probably the first to thoroughly explore the west side, including the Hoh River Valley, was the great hunter and trapper Peter Fisher, who came from the San Juan Islands in 1860 and built a trapper's cabin on the Forks Prairie. As with others of his profession, Fisher's presence in the early days was transient, so the villagers of the remote Hoh Valley felt no settlement pressure through most of the 1880s.

This was not the case for the rest of the region, and Governor Stevens, of the newly minted Washington Territory (1853), was given orders from the other Washington instructing him to sign treaties with all tribes posthaste. Under the terms of the Treaty of Olympia (1855-1856), the six-million-acre homeland of the Quileute and Hoh was ceded to the federal government and both tribes were to move to the Quinault Reservation.

Negotiations were carried out in Chinook; however, the 500-word trading language turned out to be wholly inadequate for a document so consequential. From the beginning, tribal leaders claimed they had given up no land or rights in the treaty and furthermore, those chiefs appointed by Stevens and his agents had no signing authority. As far as the Hohs were concerned, the treaty guaranteed peace with white settlers but went no further. So when the time came to move, they refused, and on September 11, 1893, the government relented in part and President Grover Cleveland set aside the Hoh Reservation at the river's mouth.

This move came just in time to avoid conflict because by the 1890s, settlers had begun to arrive in the Hoh Valley. In 1882 a white settler had been killed on the Hoh. The perpetrator was alleged to be "Doctor" Obi, a Quileute medicine man. Before Obi was found out, he very nearly killed Dan Pullen, a settler and trader, in an ambush. "Doctor" Obi went to territorial prison in Steilacoom, where he killed his cellmate in a bid to make points with his captors. It is a tribute to both settlers and Natives that, other than this incident, the settlement of the Hoh proceeded in a peaceful and orderly manner.

The Huelsdonk families, the Fisher brothers, Billy Snell, Enoch Burgess, Pete Brandeberry, Moritz, Pete Willoughby, Stodick, Kobe Kobedlin, Kuhn, H. O. Milboarn, Bill Schlensker, Otis Crippen, T. R. Schmidt, and others settled the Upper Hoh, while Toby Saux, Bill Gaul, the Elliotts, Matt Langseth, Jake Landrum, the Fletchers, the Andersons, and Captain Hank made their homes on the Lower Hoh. Houses were log cabins or hand-split cedar or spruce structures.

Gnarled and knobby ribs of ancient red cedars

River, red alders,
and Sitka spruces
in winter

One creative settler hollowed out about 40 feet of a 17-foot-diameter windfall and put a woodshed at one end and a cow stall with hay at the other, with a living space in the middle.

The Hoh Valley was a harsh place for even the toughest of men. Many left, discouraged with "proving up" on their homestead claims; some, Bill Gaul included, were lured north by Alaska gold; some couldn't pay their taxes; for others, the solitude and long, cold, wet winters aggravated quirks of personality to the point of madness. One settler rigged a booby trap to catch an imaginary enemy and fell fatally victim to his own cleverness. Elsewhere on the Upper Hoh, Enoch Burgess's tormented mind imagined that his neighbor, a man named Stodick, had become the high priest of an evil cult and Stodick's house its temple. Burgess dragged Stodick out of bed one night, choking and beating him, then with a butcher knife chased Stodick six miles to the Huelsdonk settlement. Constable Chris Morgenroth was called and Burgess, entertained by a mirror and a comb for his big full red beard, was escorted to the state institution at Steilacoom.

Life was just as lonely and hard for women. Their husbands would often be gone for weeks or even months at a time working in the Puget Sound logging camps. One local woman expressed the feelings of many when she proclaimed, "God forgive a man that brings a woman to this place for he knows not what he does."

Most early men and women were not able to endure the challenges of life on the Hoh. Lena Huelsdonk Fletcher (daughter of John Huelsdonk) in her unpublished memoirs attempted to explain why:

The early settlers of the west slope of the Olympic Peninsula came from all over the world and also from most areas of the U.S. They were of course of all stratas [sic] of society including even a Lord from England, and some well educated professional men. Very few were incompetent; they simply could not cope with what the frontier imposed: endless efforts, endless hardships, horrible discomforts, and deprivations. Most in the end could not take it.

There were, however, a few that thrived. Pete Willoughby, a hunter of considerable reputation, settled at the foot of what is now called Schmidt's Hill. Even in old age, with hands so shaky he couldn't hold a cup of coffee steady,

Pete never missed a shot. Billy Snell, a wealthy Englishman who settled downriver from Pete Willoughby, ignored his mother's pleas to return to his homeland, married a Quinault, went Native, declared himself an Indian, and eventually moved to Tahola (on the Quinault Reservation).

Pete Brandeberry, who settled upriver from John Huelsdonk (near the present park boundary), made a career with the Forest Service while also making a name for himself as a hunter and trapper. In the late 1880s Captain Hank, whose 30-foot *Surf Duck* plied the waters from Hood Canal to the Columbia, was one of the earliest to stake a claim on the Hoh. Subsequently, in 1891 his deckhand Isaac Anderson claimed land near the mouth of the river on its north side. The Henry Fletcher family came in 1896, most aboard the *Surf Duck*. Their cattle were driven overland by Henry and his son Bert. Henry's son Fred was later credited with discovering oil on the Lower Hoh. Fred found a place where a bear, to escape insects, had been wallowing in a seep. A railroad survey crew in the area was informed of the find and the rush began. Unfortunately, Oil City never did live up to its name.

Of those who came, thrived, and lived out their days on the river, none loom larger in the history, tradition, and myth of the Olympic Peninsula than John Huelsdonk and his wife, Dora, whom he brought to the remote upper reaches of the Hoh in 1892. All conversations on the subject of John begin with the "Stove with 50 pounds of flour in the oven packed 30 miles from Forks to the Hoh" story, which has been retold scores of times in books and magazines and a thousand times over by old-timers. It is firmly embedded in the legend of the state. Though in 100 years of telling, John Huelsdonk's physical exploits have grown to Bunyanesque proportions, the verifiable facts of his life need no exaggeration to become the stuff of legend.

John was the midwife for the birth of his four daughters and saw to their education at the University of Washington. When he worked off-farm for tuition or taxes, he insisted on double pay because he habitually did the work of two men. John was a hunter and trapper with few, if any, equals on the peninsula. He had the scars to prove that more than once he had gone toe to toe with a bear or cougar.

Rainbow over Huelsdonk Ridge

John's strength and endurance were exceeded only by the kind hospitality the couple showed travelers from the "outside," a place Dora ventured to only twice after first coming to the Hoh.

Now, in another century, all traces of the Native fish camps have vanished from the Hoh. Most signs of the homesteading era have vanished. Captain Hank and his brave little *Surf Duck* are at the bottom of the Pacific. The big timber is mostly gone from the lower river, and only fragments remain of the old pioneer puncheon trail. But in the Valley of the Hoh River, the Thunderbird still speaks from the snows of Mount Olympus, his scouts still on patrol. Along the river, bark-harvest marks on old cedars indicate the presence of an ancient Native culture, and in a small meadow far up the river, a sturdy little weathered cabin stands in testimony to the strength and courage of those earliest frontiersmen and -women to live on its banks.

Ancient Caterpillar,
Forks Timber Museum

Old wheel,

Forks Timber Museum

Imprints

Heidi Henkel Sinclair, Poet, Executive, The Gates Foundation

The soil shaved by Hoh River rain
washes away from roots, now crests
the land where your chickens feed
you, dressed in winter skirts
your boots dig into swamp moss
leave imprints of your iron

boot nails, where your father, Iron
Man of the Hoh, left his muddy rain
mark, footprints pressed into moss.
moss like a disease crests
branches and earth, skirts
fir trees, gives deer winter feed

and dry feed
for summer sparrow nests, to iron
wings and shelter children under skirts
keep them dry from rain
splattering the Olympic Crests
leaving patches of moss.

Morning light, bigleaf
maples with licorice
fern and club moss

Your father, buried in moss
slept where your chickens feed
cradled between mountain crests
his pillow carved from cliffs of iron
ore. He rose, showered in stinging glacier rain,
slipped into Quinault skirts

then he danced, like a white man, skirt-
ing death, he leaped on the moss,
scattered clouds of rain
like chicken feed
and he, River Hoh's man of iron
stamped his mark on Indian crests

where now the glazed snow of Mount Olympus crests
their cedar-bark skirts.
you, daughter of iron
climb mountains of peat moss
stitched with chicken feed
and Hoh River rain,

to pay homage to father of iron, pioneer of Olympic crests
buried in moss, the Rain Forest feed.
You turn away daughter, lifting rain splattered skirts.

Written for Mrs. Charles Lewis in memory of her father, John Huelsdonk. This poem is a sestina inspired by a picture of Mrs. Lewis that appeared in the Seattle Times.

Decayed cascara leaves
on alder bark

Raccoon tracks on river sand

Calligraphic tracks
and traces in river silt

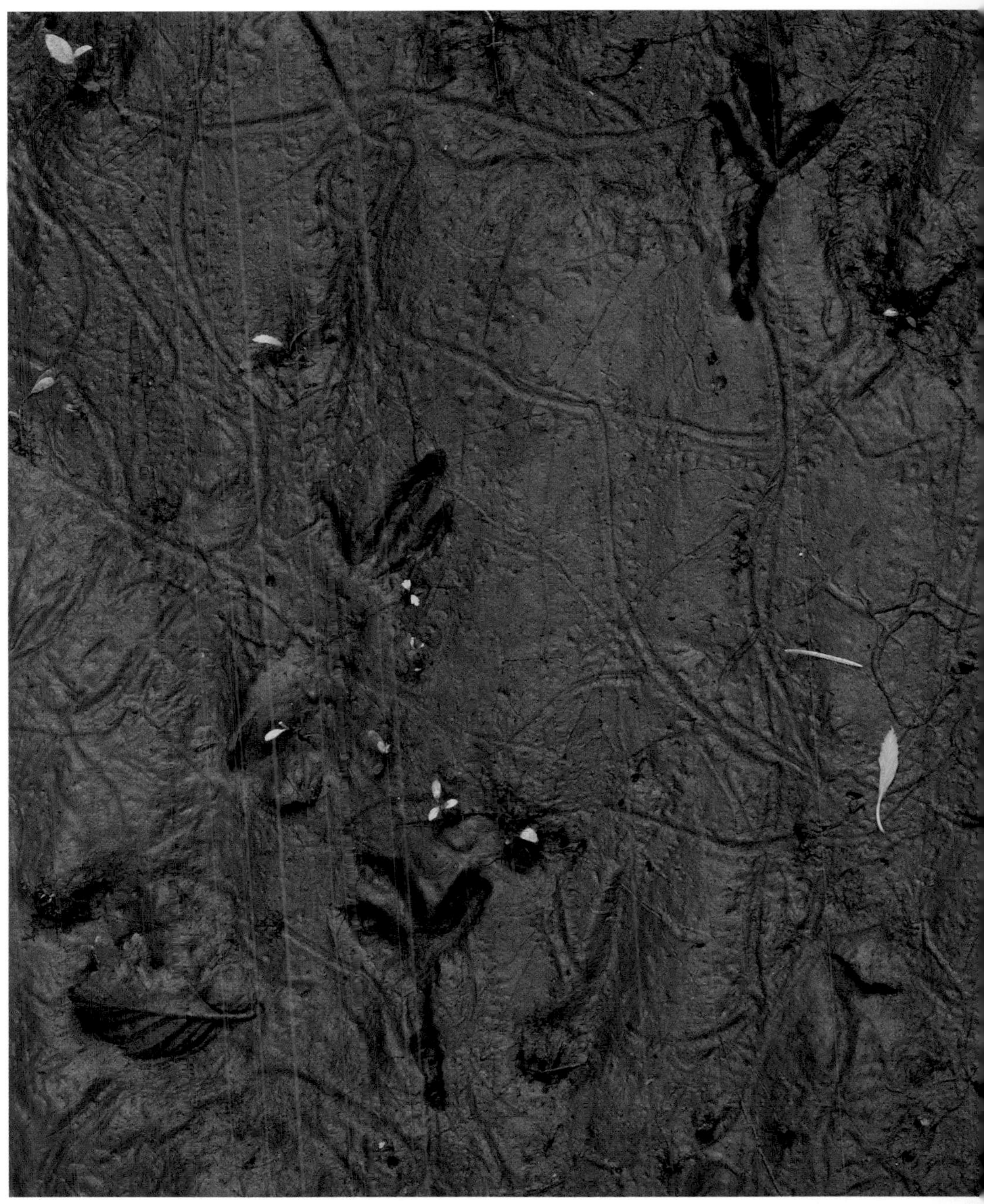

A Stewardship Legacy

by John C. Richmond, Hoh Valley Resident

A point in my early memory, ca. 1938-1950, is a snapshot of those times. Old-growth timber stood on the hillsides; elk herds were nearly inaccessible to tribal and sports hunters. Farms in the valley grazed over 600 cattle on the open range, yet salmon darkened the side channels of the river. Set-net fishing was practiced on the south half of the river on the reservation. Nearly every small tributary had pairs of spawning salmon along its length, to surprisingly steep gradients and shallow depths.

A life experience, which grows with time into an ideal of one's existence, is often an appreciation of a life near nature. This appreciation is reinforced by the physical exertion, sweat, blood, and tears paid for the experience on a daily basis, for the privilege of survival under exposure to harsh conditions. Eden is in many places. I have camped in the tropical jungle, having even more rain than the Hoh, with the people of Micronesia, close to the land, working to preserve their natural resource values, and have visited the pastoral scenes of New Zealand. Most cherished, however, is the ability to seek solace in the familiar and beautiful land of one's lifetime. Such is why the residents of the Hoh River Valley have endured their chosen life.

A week ago, beginning at a place of my earliest memory of the Hoh River, at the canoe landing on the southerly side, I retraced a path once familiar, now obscured by vegetation. The deep ruts and the wooden sled used to transport supplies to the house are gone. Once familiar maples and tall cottonwoods have decayed, fallen, and become the soil of the bottomland. Coming one-quarter mile into the homestead clearing, still occupied and farmed, where the house stands, the memories of eventful occurrences of more than 69 years are recalled.

"Ironman" John Huelsdonk's Hoh River homestead in spring

This homestead is where my grandfather John Huelsdonk and my grandmother Dora raised four daughters, the second eldest also named Dora, being my mother, born in 1895. All had chores and responsibilities, while being educated at home by contract teachers through grade and high school. Two attained college degrees and were in turn hired to live and teach in homes of students.

Tasks for Grandpa were typical of the time and in addition included earning money by backpacking supplies, fur trapping and hunting predators, pulling the dugout canoe to safety before high water, and the host of other chores required for survival. Grandma performed the typical tasks of housekeeping and raising the girls.

Mother, living at home between teaching assignments, did tasks such as trapping and hunting, shearing the sheep, mending fences, and bucking logs out of the trail to Forks with a seven-foot crosscut saw after the 1921 hurricane.

I was four years old. I remember Dad taking me to catch my first fish on the river, at the mouth of Owl Creek. I told him that I had hooked the bottom of the river. It was a 14-inch Dolly Varden, harvesting eggs from a spring chinook redd.

In the fall of 1943, on the Hoh with all its pleasant isolation, Grandpa was digging potatoes, shaking the sticky soil from them as best he could with the wide-tined spading fork. Much of the clayey soil would cling to the potatoes, which he would rub clean with his bare hands before placing them in a bucket and carrying them to the spring to rinse clean, then put them in the wheelbarrow to take to the root cellar in the barn.

I was about to be given a most important lesson. I asked him why he did not just wash off all the dirt in the spring water. He told me that it took a long time to get good garden soil and it needed to be saved; the river had enough mud from the glacier, anyway.

He said, "You must practice soil conservation."

Arable soils exist where sediments, without stones, were deposited in the floodplains as the glaciers receded. With careful tilling and heritage seeds selected for climatic suitability, a reliable and safe source of produce was established and maintained.

Animal products were hot canned, dried, or smoked, and included homegrown beef, mutton, and poultry. Wild game in season was venison, elk, and fish. There was no risk of contamination from sprays, chemicals, or antibiotics.

In the summer of 1943 after the hay was put into the barn, Aunt Bettine and two teenage cousins, Mother, brother Dave, and I went on a camping trip to Blue Glacier, using one saddle horse and two packhorses. Not another person was in that area all summer. Cougar tracks dominated the trail. Good to get back home.

That year, after automobile access, many people would look at the 200-foot-tall trees and the 20 or so hand-cleared acres, wanting to buy only a few acres on which to erect a cabin. Land is too precious to sell for mere money. All offers were rejected. Even today, we struggle with those outsiders like the Hoh River Trust who have purchased land in the valley with the proclamation of doing good. But as we discover shared values, we may find common ground on the stewardship of the Hoh River. Time will tell.

Ruffed grouse drumming on a log

Tiers of old-growth forest in spring

The Upper Hoh family cemetery represents five generations. The family cemetery on the Lower Hoh includes a Native American. Tribal cemeteries exist near the river's mouth. All have become sacred ground, regardless of ethnicity.

Earnest, honest, and concerned residents, occupying this lovely valley, have a mission. It is to preserve the cultural community, traditional heritage, future legacy, and long-term productivity of the Hoh River Valley. We seek to maintain the balance of wildlife, agriculture, tourism, forest management, and rural self-sufficiency by continuing and furthering the individual stewardship of the families living in the valley.

Our goals are clear. We will raise and educate our children in a safe and productive environment. We will continue to produce safe and nutritious food for hundreds of families, as has been done for over 100 years on Hoh River farms and ranches. We will promote a friendly environment for land and river wildlife, and provide the facilities for tourism, for education, and for recreation, thus supporting the local area economy. We will enable the ecologically sound and scientific harvest and reproduction of forest products. Collectively we will provide a tax base to support community necessities such as roads, schools, hospitals, fire protection, and local government.

The role of the land-vested steward thus is to be an integral part of the environment. This is achieved only after successful survival from the elements and predations of wildlife, and ensuring harmony with the rest of nature. This stewardship attitude is maintained by most of the descendants of the pioneer settlers on the Olympic Peninsula.

People who live on the land care for the land.

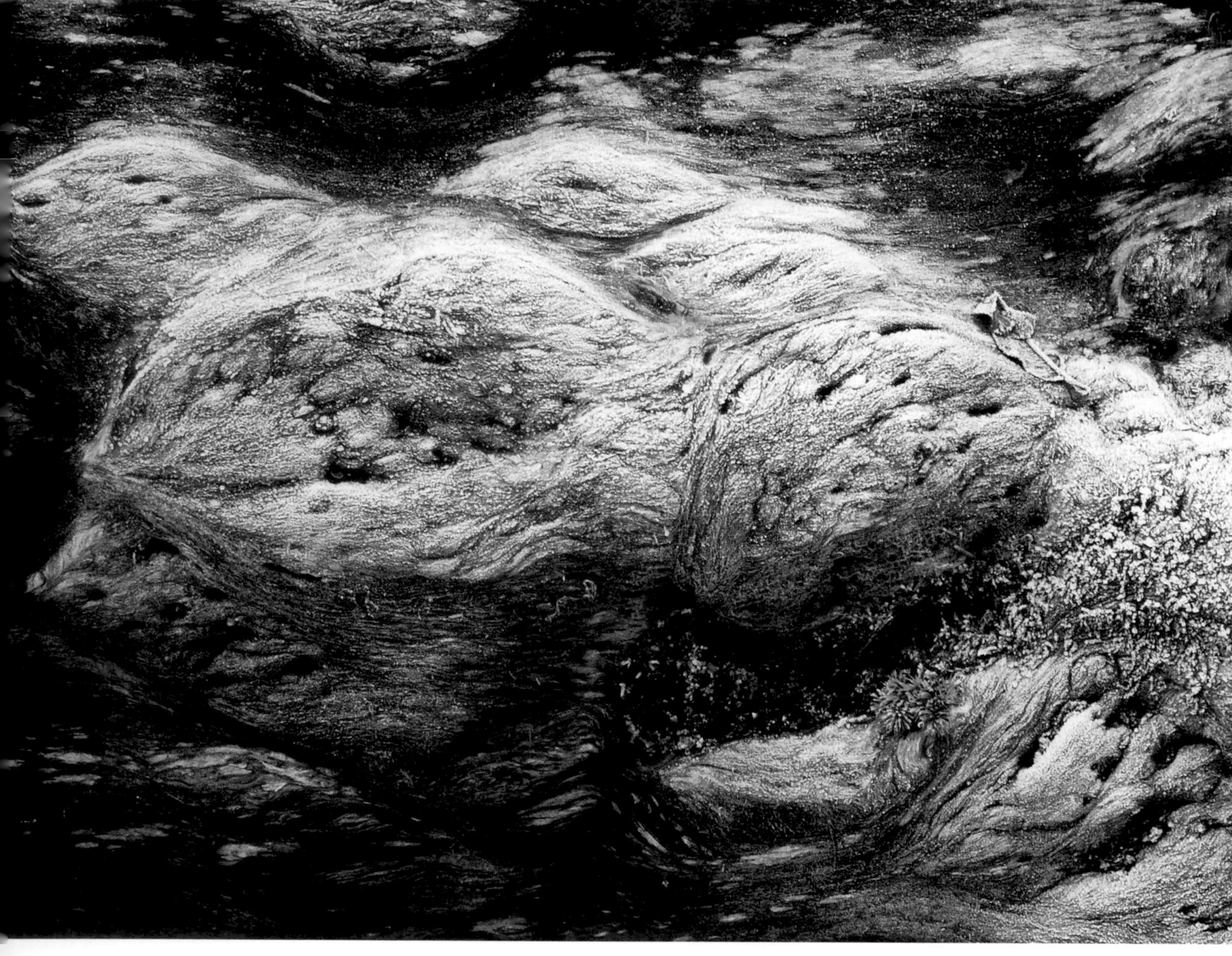

Frost on weathered log

Buttercup through horsetail

Mother Hoh

by Nedra Reed, Mayor, Forks, Washington

"It's a monster, Grandpa!!!" These were the words of my eight-year-old grandson, the quintessential "city kid" sent out to the country in Forks to spend time with his grandparents. He is the second generation of fishermen "growing up on the Hoh River" in our family who was having the chance to fish waters that his grandpa, grandma, and dad have fished for decades. He too was enjoying the incredible beauty of one of the peninsula's wonders and had on his line one of the Hoh's prized salmon.

That day, the "monster" threw the hook, and swam majestically up the river. While it would have been released anyway, it was a good opportunity to turn a "lost fish" into an educational discussion for which grandparents are always known. There along the banks of one of this state's most remarkable rivers, the stage was set for a long talk with our grandson regarding our responsibility to preserve our God-given resources, the mystery of the salmon, and even life itself.

Our Native American friends have millennia of experience and association with the Hoh. The rest of us have all come to develop a special place in our hearts and lives for this area. Although the river has seen many changes, it still remains somewhat a mystery. Depending on the snowmelt or storms, it can run the color of a milky jade green to the darkest chocolate brown. Sometimes the cause of the color change occurs so far back in the headwaters, few of us know what to attribute it to. Every year it chooses to move, quite frankly, where it wants to, and all man's efforts to harness it have failed.

The river has seen many political battles and has remained relatively unscathed throughout them all. It's easy for folks to rattle these off in a typical "West End matter-of-fact" way: the fish controversy during the Boldt Decision; the logging controversy regarding the spotted owl since the 1990s; and now the issue of preserving it for nature to do with as she feels.

Daisies and grasses, lower Hoh River

I must admit I was very concerned when the Hoh River Trust first came to our attention. Rumors were rampant: "Property rights of residents will be threatened"; "The river accesses will be closed"; "You won't be allowed to fish near land owned by the Trust"; and on and on.

We all made mistakes during this time. We failed to communicate to each other our plans, our concerns, and our fears. That failure could easily be attributed to the legacy of the 1990s and the "war in the woods" that swirled about the trees lining the Hoh and elsewhere on the West End.

We Peninsulaites are very independent, opinionated, and some would say difficult at times. Every day those of us living here are confronted by a host of challenges—some weather caused, some policy caused—that have a direct impact on the economic vitality and stability of our community. All that said, we also do care for our environment, our quality of life, and the wonderful places like the Hoh River Valley. Sure, some things about the way land is managed and controlled in the valley will continue to be a point of contention. However, we also know that a community can only truly be a community if all of its members learn to work together for the greater collective good.

While we all find better ways of doing that, we can be assured that Mother Hoh will continue to meander and flow where she wants. That the elk will continue to wade across the gravel bars of her banks. Eagles will continue to soar through the dew-thickened air over trees covered in lichens and moss. Steelhead and salmon will continue to make their way back . . . to the river. In those wonders of nature, we will all find the same inspiration that re-creates that wonder of discovery enjoyed by my grandson many years ago. Hopefully, working together we can ensure that that same wonder is discovered by future generations for centuries.

Band of Roosevelt elk
crossing the river

Salmon Sanctuary

by Phil Wallin, Western Rivers Conservancy

In 1892, Livingston Stone, one of the founders of the American Fisheries Society, proposed a system of salmon sanctuaries that would "protect wild salmonids from the effects of development and a burgeoning Northwest population." The Klamath on California's north coast was proposed as a prototype, but instead it went the way of hydropower dams, irrigation, industrial logging, and massive fish die-offs.

While no system of official salmon sanctuaries has ever been established, private organizations have been working quietly and tirelessly to create *unofficial* sanctuaries on our best remaining salmon and steelhead streams. The idea is to protect a few rivers where scientists can see how a whole, healthy river ecosystem works, from headwaters to ocean. These rivers could serve as genetic "savings accounts" for Pacific salmonids from which rivers could be restocked if climate change or other catastrophes extirpate native runs.

These sanctuaries should not all be in Alaska and Siberia. A few of them should be in the lower 48 if they are to help our native runs survive. They should be protected from top to bottom.

The Hoh River is a perfect example of a salmon sanctuary. It is a small, wet watershed with pristine headwaters that are fully protected within Olympic National Park. It is one of a cluster of high-quality salmon streams that flow from the Olympics to the Pacific, and the Hoh boasts the healthiest wild salmon runs in the lower 48 states.

In 2001, Western Rivers Conservancy took on the challenge of securing protection for the riparian zone on the Hoh River downstream from Olympic National Park, including key tributaries. Our specialty is land acquisition. Simply put, we buy critical habitat lands along the most outstanding rivers in the West and transfer those lands into permanent conservation stewardship.

South Fork Hoh River in spring

We saw the Hoh River as an opportunity to protect nearly an entire healthy river ecosystem. The headwaters and upper basin (over 60 percent of the Hoh watershed) are protected by the national park, so there is a dependable source of clean, cold water. There are no dams. There are no major water diversions. There is no significant hatchery influence. There is a dynamic, complex floodplain with a healthy riparian forest and good gravel recruitment. The estuary is relatively natural. All 13 species of native salmonids are present. While the river will benefit greatly from some restoration measures, it is a fundamentally healthy system that mainly needs protection and good management.

Conservation doesn't happen in a social vacuum. It was clear to us that the community on the western Olympic Peninsula would not support federal ownership and management of the lower Hoh River. Many residents still regard the Olympic National Park as a recent federal land-grab. If the Lower Hoh was to become a salmon sanctuary, it would have to be done through private action and private stewardship.

Some of the lower Hoh River was already in good private stewardship, in the hands of families who had been there for generations. The Lewises, Fletchers, Petersons, Huelsdonks, Barlows, and others had managed their farms and river shoreline carefully. They were lifelong anglers and appreciated the value of the riparian forest as habitat for salmon and steelhead. Likewise, the Hoh Tribe for thousands of years had made their home along the river and had relied on its bounty for sustenance and cultural identity. The Tribe had been a strong voice for a healthy and productive ecosystem.

However, most of the Hoh River lands were owned by three entities: the Washington Department of Natural Resources, Rayonier Timberlands, and CalPERS, the California public employees pension fund. All these lands, which totaled over 70 percent of the river corridor outside the park boundary, were managed for timber production, within the limits of state and federal laws. With alder becoming valuable for saw-logs as well as pulp, the riparian zone would be under greater pressure than in the past.

Leaping wild
coho salmon

Owl Creek between winter storms

We believed that the "highest and best use" of the riparian zone was to produce salmon and support other species habitat, not for timber harvest or private development. The only way to show this, we believed, was to purchase these lands. Because the Hoh was famous as a salmon and steelhead stream, we believed that the funding would be available from both public and private sources for land purchases, given the tremendous momentum that has been building over the years to protect these dwindling icons of the Pacific Northwest.

The question remained, who would manage these lands? We concluded that the best steward would be a privately constituted, privately funded, nonprofit "Hoh River Trust." We thought this could be a new kind of organization that would go beyond the traditional functions of a land trust. A river trust would not only buy and manage land and easements. It would also be a voice, and a force, for conservation of the whole river ecosystem in a way that involved and engaged the local community. In this role, the trust could work in unison with the families in the Hoh River Valley who share the same values and vision.

Fortunately we had the help and partnership of the Wild Salmon Center in forming and launching the Hoh River Trust. While we contributed the idea of the river trust, Wild Salmon Center connected us with the people who made the Hoh River Trust succeed, especially its founding chair, Bob Blais.

Unless we could buy the Hoh River lands, however, the Hoh River Trust would have nothing to manage and no "standing" as an advocate for the river. Fortunately, Western Rivers Conservancy developed a good working relationship with Rayonier Timber, the primary landowner on the Hoh. The company saw the wisdom of selling riparian lands that are hard to operate for timber production and reinvesting the money in more operable uplands elsewhere.

On December 21, 2001, we purchased the first installment of Hoh River land from Rayonier, which included the confluence of the Hoh with Winfield and Elk Creeks, two top-priority spawning streams. In three additional purchases in 2003 and 2004, we bought all the remaining lands on the Hoh owned by Rayonier, including the confluence with the South Fork Hoh. We borrowed the funds for these purchases from three different foundations.

Following the leadership of Congressman Norm Dicks, we approached the U.S. Fish and Wildlife Service for funds to enable the Hoh River Trust to purchase the lands from us. Thanks largely to the efforts of Congressman Dicks, the Hoh River Project received a series of three grants through Section 6 of the Endangered Species Act totaling nearly $9 million. These grants enabled WRC to convey 4,450 acres of land to the Hoh River Trust in two installments in 2005 and 2006. In the meantime, the Hoh River Trust had developed the expertise, resources, and infrastructure to manage these lands capably for fish, wildlife, and people.

The concept of a nonprofit conservation organization buying the Hoh River corridor was controversial on the west side of the Olympic Peninsula. Some people feared that we would lock up lands that had traditionally been open to hunting, fishing, and floating, or believed that we were a proxy for the National Park Service. After many meetings and conversations, and most importantly after the Hoh River Trust began to manage the lands in an open and reasonable way, the controversy eased.

We still face the challenge of acquiring the remaining 3,000 acres of Hoh River land owned by another industrial forestry company. In all likelihood this will require that we purchase timberlands that can then be exchanged for these lands. As in all conservation work, the key to success is patience and persistence. Western Rivers Conservancy is committed to this process to make certain that the Hoh River Trust has the lands needed to ensure the essential ecological functions of the Hoh River.

We are fortunate that we have had stalwart help from so many partners: the Wild Salmon Center, Washington State Department of Natural Resources, the U.S. Fish and Wildlife Service, the David and Lucile Packard Foundation, the Bullitt Foundation, the Paul G. Allen Forest Protection Foundation, and the Wildlife Forever Fund, to mention a few. Above all, we have benefited from the solid commitment and support of Congressman Norm Dicks, who has kept us all on course. These people and organizations have given us the staying power we need to accomplish the long-term goal: permanent conservation stewardship over our Hoh River lands.

We believe that the Hoh River project can serve as a model for the nation in many ways. It is a model of a sanctuary that encompasses an entire river ecosystem. It is a model of private nonprofit land stewardship with strong local collaboration. It is a model for the use of both private and public capital for land conservation. It is a model of cooperation with the forest products industry. It is a model for integrating river conservation with the cultural, economic, and recreational needs and values of a local community. And finally, it is a model for the power of a vision when that vision is pursued with patience, persistence, imagination, and cooperation.

Kayakers rounding the bend, Hoh River

A Life in the Hoh River Valley

by Lloyd J. Allen,
Founder, Allen Logging Company

I was born in Oregon, and went straight to the woods right out of high school, logging alder with a horse. After a year or two, I started hauling logs with a truck. I hauled for a year or so, and worked pretty hard at it.

The operation that I hauled for had a sawmill, and they had this timber, and a little piece left over that they wanted someone to log. I asked the mill owner about it and he said, "If you want to log that, you can. And if you work as hard at it as you do hauling logs, you'll be successful." So I got that job—and I lost money on it! But the next year, I ran the Cat myself, and I started making money then. I think that made a strong impression on me. You often have to do things yourself.

I managed a few trips up here from Oregon before 1948 and I liked the looks of the country. At that time, there was not much logged-off ground up here—pretty primitive area. For me it was either here or Alaska. My wife, Bertha, knew when she married me that she might be living out in the woods. She said, "That's OK."

There weren't any mills in the Hoh area when I came. We had some success with logging the Burn (the Forks fire of 1951), then started a veneer mill, which we converted to a sawmill a few years later. But we've seen lots of mills come and go over time; better mills than this one! We were a smaller operation, and we always made a lot of chips here for paper mills as well as lumber. That allowed us some flexibility and helped us survive the ups and downs.

Many of our customers have come and gone over the years as well. We have always tried to stay ahead of it. We are fortunate that we were always able to find new customers when we needed them. We've kept at it for a long time now. Today, we have around 50 people working here. We keep it pretty stable, mostly local people. A lot of the folks are longtime employees, many of them now retiring. We've got second-generation folks, and maybe even third.

You have to enjoy your work to do it for so long. I have. I'm 90 years old and still come to work most days.

Old Sitka spruce in spring

I've spent a lot of time fishing on the Hoh, especially on a Saturday afternoon. I don't catch many fish these days, but I used to catch a few cutthroat in the fall after the salmon would go up into Winfield Creek. Beautiful fish, and good eating. I enjoy eating them just as much as I do catching them. Now, I don't know if you can even keep them. Long ago I began to do a little fly-fishing and I learned that that was the only way to go.

I've been down the Hoh by boat as well a number of times. Not always safely! There is a rough spot over here where the water drops. I had bought a rubber raft from Sears Roebuck and tried it out with my dog. We were over-full, and when we went down that drop, my dog went out the front. Fortunately I was able to pull him in farther downriver.

I ended up loaning out that rubber boat to two fellows in the shop one Saturday, and a few hours later one of them caught a ride back and he was soaking wet. "Ken's gone, he's drowned," this one fellow says. He tells me they hadn't gone a hundred yards when they both started paddling on the same side of the boat. They went in circles right into a logjam and capsized the boat. This was shocking news to us. Ken was married, with children. We didn't hardly know what to do, but we knew we couldn't just leave Ken in the river. So my logging foreman and I got some rope and set off for this logjam about three miles upriver. And then here comes Ken, walking down the river pulling that boat. Apparently he had swum after that boat as it was floating away from the logjam. He said all he could see was dollar signs floating down the river, so he had to save the boat. I've never loaned a boat out since. But I do still have one out there in the shed, and I think on these long summer evenings that I'm going to take it out again, maybe with my dog, but I haven't had a chance yet.

I enjoy the drive from Port Angeles, around Lake Crescent: beautiful sunrises and sunsets. Ordinarily, I headed out of P.A. at about 5 a.m. and got back about 6 p.m. My wife liked me to be home by 6 for supper. And I decided that as long as I can do that, well, I'd just as soon not retire. She passed away in March, so I stay out here now every other night or so. Tonight I'm staying here in Forks. When I'm up in P.A., I have some friends who cook me a nice meal. I've also got three daughters that want to make sure I'm not lonely, three good son-in-laws, and grandsons and granddaughters. But they don't have much interest in this kind of life. They are looking toward what their moms and dads have done: law, and teaching. Now that's a pretty good life, too.

I've never thought about moving somewhere else. No. I don't think I could find any place that suited me as well as this Hoh River Valley. Not too much snow, I don't like hot weather particularly, and I don't mind the rain. There are lots of good things to say about this place.

Lloyd Allen and Bingo with one of his favorite trees

Snags and new growth after 1978 Hoh burn

Hoh River flows
through a logjam

Alien Fish Camp

(from *The Fisherman's Prayer*)

by Pat Neal, Writer, River Guide

And so, another salmon season passes dead astern. I hope you did better than I did, huddled by the stove, trying to dry out a soaked hide—mine. Waiting for the landfill to open so I can dump what's left of a woodsman's kit 30 years in the making, before one more so-called fishing buddy drops by to observe: "You sure know how to build a campfire . . . ha-ha."

Tent camping in the monsoon season of the Olympic Peninsula rain forest can be a thrilling nature experience. When the wind hits the old-growth timber, bad things start falling out of the sky. Treetops bigger than a telephone pole can bust off and plow into the forest floor like a giant spear. Slabs of loose bark and broken limbs can fly hundreds of yards through the air in the wind. Or the whole tree, along with a bunch of its neighbors, can simply blow over.

With wind comes the rain. A tropical Pacific rain can blow in and melt the new snow for many thousands of feet up the mountains. The creeks become rivers, and the rivers become war zones of big trees plowing their way downstream like a big wood highway.

This can happen so fast, you can wake up in the river if you don't watch where you camp. Lying awake all night listening to the roar of the rising river and the frightening crash of big timber hitting the ground is enough to make you wish for an abduction by aliens. But we camp in the monsoons anyway. The salmon run upstream on the high water. You want to be on the river in the fall when the river is dropping and clearing from mud brown to emerald green.

I drove up the Hoh River Valley looking for a place to camp. Any given day on the Hoh River in the fall can be the best fishing there is. I drove to the end of an old grade and walked out a short way to look at the river.

A bald eagle sat in a snag at the head of a long, slow drift, staring down between his feet. A king salmon rolled like a small torpedo half out of the river.

Hoh River, autumn fog

When the kings run upriver in the fall, the rest of the fish—the coho, steelhead, and sea-run cutthroat—run with them. We just call them all bluebacks to avoid confusion.

I figured that if I set up my tent quickly, I could catch a nice salmon before dark. I went to work in a patch of small trees, lashing together the classic fish camp with all the trimmings.

Nothing beats a bough bed for comfort in the wilderness. Constructed properly, a bough bed is sturdy yet springy, and it smells terrific. After sleeping, eating seems to be the next-most-popular camp activity. It helps to have a well-organized folding camp kitchen. There are many fine ones on the market. I found a wire rope spool sitting in the landing of an old logging show, set a gas stove and some boxes on top, and that was the kitchen.

Once you rig the camp kitchen, you'll want to begin work on the restroom facilities. Latrine placement is crucial on a dark and stormy night. Your facilities should be waterproof, with a door snug enough to keep the skunks out. They don't like to be surprised.

I camped in a grove of second-growth timber. Within the grove was the dark hulk of a monolithic stump more than a dozen feet high and at least eight feet in diameter—all that was left of a tree more than 200 feet tall. It might have been about 500 years old.

The Olympic Peninsula rain forest grows the biggest spruces in the world. Spruce was used for building airplanes back in World War I. Only the best trees with clear wood and straight grain were used. That was hand logging at its finest. The loggers climbed up a massive spruce by standing on spring-boards, planks set in notches chipped in the side of the tree. They might have had to climb above the butt swell, where it would be easier to cut the giant down with nothing but an ax and a crosscut saw. There's a lot of pitch in a big spruce stump. The old loggers packed kerosene to keep the saw from gumming up in the cut while they were sawing.

It must have been quite a sight to watch the big spruce go over. The fallers would have been 10 feet up the stump when the tree started falling. Once they got

Mosses with boot

the tree on the ground, the real work started. They bucked the logs to length and split them into beams, called "cants," with wedges pounded by a heavy log sledge suspended on a tripod. They wrestled the cants to the river and floated them down to the mouth, where some captain courageous boomed them out through the surf of the open Pacific Ocean—all for the war effort.

That old spruce stump was more than just a historic monument. It was a perfect back wall for my camp. I rigged a pole from the tent to the stump and lashed on a tarp.

By the time I got things set up, it was too dark to fish. I heard splashing down at the river. It might have been the salmon jumping or elk crossing the river. Whatever it was, I was camped in the right spot. It stopped raining.

Last misty light on the river

The stars came out, so I started a small campfire and sat out to watch them. Building a campfire in a soggy November in the Hoh Rain Forest is no easy job. As soon as a piece of dead wood hits the ground, it soaks up enough water to start growing moss and sprouting mushrooms. Your only chance of building a fire in these woods is to find some dry pitch or bring along some fire starter.

I had thought of everything in this camp, even dry cedar kindling from home. I sat and listened to the river and stared into the flames. For a moment, there was a feeling of such peace and contentment, to be in a snug camp in country loaded with fish and game.

Then a small root attached to the massive spruce stump caught fire. I thought that was a handy bit of good luck. It would save on the firewood packing. I built up the fire to a cheery blaze.

As the flames climbed higher, the surface of the stump appeared moist. I thought it was wet from the rain, but I was wrong. The moisture was melting pitch running down the stump. The big spruce must have been cut in the spring when the sap was running. Once the tree was cut, the sap coagulated in the stump until it fossilized. I now know there must have been enough pitch in that stump to fill a dump truck. Suddenly, the melted pitch caught on fire. In just a few minutes, the entire stump erupted into a wall of flames. It showered my tent with a blizzard of red-hot cinders.

I grabbed an ax and started chopping poles and slashing ropes, trying to rip my camp apart before it burned down. The flames leaped higher.

In no time, the stump looked like a rocket stuck in the ground. Little trees burst into flames. The moss was catching on fire. I ran around, beating out flames with a shovel.

Daylight revealed a scene of awesome devastation. There was a smoking crater where the spruce stump had been, and a melted outhouse. Some nosy road hunters stopped by and wanted to know what happened.

"There is only one explanation," I said. "Alien abduction."

River Bird

(from *The Fisherman's Prayer*)

by Pat Neal

I saw a river bird out on a mighty stream.
Her call was barely heard, a whisper in a dream.
Enjoying this as all her days, fluttering
Through a tortured maze
Of white water pounding statues of black rock.
Being near to drowning, I was transfixed in shock.
That such a frail and feathered thing
Should live a life of ease,
In such tumultuous surroundings,
Is encouraging to me.

Dipper in autumn

reflection

Silty river after
heavy rains

Hob River in spring

Hooked by the Hoh

by JD Love, Fishing Guide

My fondest childhood memories are linked to the Hoh River. I'll never forget my first trip to the Hoh with my dad. It was famous for its fall run of jack salmon in those days. I can still hear the incessant splashing of those fish powering through the shallow riffles as I lay in my sleeping bag eagerly awaiting daylight.

I remember sneaking out of the tent early one morning with my spinning rod in hand and fishing a nearby pool on the river. By the time I was done working that hole, I had pulled out a steelhead, a king salmon, and a big Dolly Varden. Although I didn't know it at the time, those early experiences would ultimately influence my decision to make a life on the rivers of the Olympic Peninsula.

I became a fishing guide almost 30 years ago, when I realized that I could have more impact on people's understanding of the natural world and the importance of respecting our river resources as a guide than slogging through the politics of fish management as an underling in the state's Department of Natural Resources. So I set up shop in Forks in 1979, guiding during the salmon and steelhead seasons on the Olympic Peninsula that ran from October through May. My summers were spent guiding in Alaska and then in Montana, but ultimately we settled our family in the Forks community and became year-round residents over 20 years ago.

The Hoh is renowned for its wild winter steelhead and its fall salmon, but what I love is the variety of fish you can encounter in the summer. I've caught humpies and chums in it every year, though they are not very abundant. It's mainly a chinook and coho river, and then summer steelhead, bull trout, and sea-run cutthroat. And there's something to be said for that comfortable summer weather!

Two of the biggest changes that I've witnessed over the years are the increasing interest in chasing these prized fish with a fly rod and a greater tendency toward catch-and-release. In the early days, probably because there were so many fish, the emphasis was on catching a limit of fish using whatever gear was most productive, as the sooner you could limit out, the sooner you got off the river, and everyone

River rocks in winter flow

was happy. It was almost to the point where if you could catch your limit in the pool where you launched your boat and then put the boat back up on the trailer, that was considered a masterful day of guiding and fishing!

Eventually, and especially when I started fishing other places, I realized that people really were not entirely satisfied with that. It became more about the experience. I think the decline in the numbers of fish has also helped the clientele to change over the years because people don't have the expectation anymore that they are going to be filling their coolers and freezers after a day of fishing on the river. Also, there are many recent arrivals to the Northwest who really want to get out and spend a day on the river, where catching a fish is a welcome bonus to the whole experience of floating the river.

And the Hoh is great for that because it's this big open glacial valley that emerges from an ancient rain forest. It's a magical setting with very little development along the banks. When you float the Hoh you have a sense that you are on a river that hasn't changed much in hundreds of years. We see elk, eagles, lots of wildlife—and on a good day we catch plenty of fish, too!

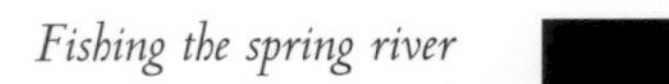
Fishing the spring river

The Hoh is constantly changing. Every year we have to relearn it as the high flows from winter's pounding storms redirect the river around its wide floodplain, depositing large trees and carving out new channels. There are certain stretches that are reasonably consistent, canyon-type sections where the fish holding spots will always be there. But on much of the lower river, last year's hot hole could be half a mile up or down river because of its ever-changing condition. There is always a sense of adventure on the Hoh.

Conservation has become a bigger issue on the Olympic Peninsula rivers, and the Hoh is certainly an important part of the equation. Private organizations like the Hoh River Trust and Western Rivers Conservancy are working to protect the Hoh from future development. Some folks have a tendency to just assume that the Hoh will always be a great river. But if we are not careful, one day we will be asking ourselves, "Where did all the fish go?" and "What happened to the habitat?"

As a guide, what I like about the Hoh is that my clients get a sense of wildness within a settled valley, the feeling of a space that is relatively unchanged. So I take people to the Hoh for the adventure of fishing a rain-forest stream, where signs of human development are at a minimum. My biggest hope for the Hoh is that these conservation efforts will preserve that sense of wild for future generations.

Even now, when I take a day off from guiding, I head out to the Hoh, filled with that same sense of thrill and anticipation I experienced camping with my dad. Not much has changed since the time of those early childhood experiences. Sure, we aren't seeing the abundance of fish that there was back then, but the river is still so special to me. It courses through that valley as it has for hundreds and thousands of years, with very little human disturbance. I consider it to be a national treasure that should be there for everyone, now and in the future. I tell people, "If you want to know what the rain forest is all about, just drive up the Hoh River Valley." I know they'll be hooked, just as I was many years ago.

The Salmon Calendar

by John McMillan and James Starr, Fish Biologists

To the attentive eye, each moment of the year has its own beauty.

— Ralph Waldo Emerson

In 2002 the west coast of the Olympic Peninsula experienced its second-driest summer on a contemporary record reaching back about 70 years. The fall rains did not arrive in the Hoh River Valley until mid-November. In most years, the rains would arrive by mid-October. This was a troubling time to many people in the Hoh watershed, especially the Native Americans who had inhabited it for thousands of years.

The problem with the low flows was that a huge run of salmon was staging in the salt water. It was the biggest run of fall chinook and coho salmon in recent memory, yet the river was too shallow for these big fish to navigate.

By late October many fish could not wait any longer, and schools of bright salmon started to ascend the lower main-stem Hoh River each night under the cover of darkness. The upstream migration, although short, was not easy. The long, shallow riffles were difficult to traverse. Inevitably, the fish made it up only a mile or two. A couple weeks after the fish began their upstream migration, thousands of salmon were stranded in pools in the lower main-stem river. Further upstream migration was impossible. There they sat for three weeks, swollen and ripe with eggs, impatient, and starting to decay. I was worried about the fish.

Eventually the rains arrived. I was sitting alongside the Lower Hoh that day. I watched as hundreds of fish skittered and splashed up through the shallow riffles. Within a few hours of steady rainfall, the river was so high that fish could no longer be seen. I knew they would be able to complete their upstream migration. As I walked back to my truck that evening, I felt a great sense of relief.

Clear flow of the South Fork Hoh River

Driving home in the rain that night, I thought about the Hoh River and the Native Americans who have lived there for thousands of years shrouded in mystery.

They are a group of noble people, like the river's fish, rugged and adaptive. Their culture evolved over thousands of years living precariously on a thin slice of rain forest flanked by a vast, cantankerous ocean to the west and the great Mount Olympus and Thunderbird to the east. The rain forest was lush with mammoth trees, elk, and fish, with all of this productivity fostered by an annual wrath of winter rains. Similar winter rains nearly drove Lewis and Clark to madness at the mouth of the Columbia. Yet these people thrived, and so did their fish. But the fish's survival was in question to some degree that year the rains did not show up on time.

Perhaps what helped the tribes cope that year and others like it was context, the knowledge that the rains would come and go, just like the fish. They shared a belief that time is not a measure of hours, days, or months, but instead a measure of biological patterns. This was, and still is, referred to as "Indian Time." This measure of time is ancient. It is simply a biological calendar. And the most influential biological pattern of the calendar is that of the salmon.

I share a soul with the Hoh Tribe in their measure of time—our calendar a reflection of the river and movements of salmon. Such a calendar is marked by fall, winter, spring, and summer, just like the calendar that hangs in our homes. However, it is also markedly different. Months are absent. The four seasons are notably indistinct.

Instead, the seasons are a mosaic of overlapping weather patterns driving the spawning, death, birth, and migration of salmon. There is no new year in the river's calendar. There is only the constant hum of life coursing downstream from mountain peaks, meandering across floodplains, and cutting its way through bedrock canyons to its inevitable junction with a vast ocean. Up and down this powerful liquid force salmon, trout, and char move each year. They are prompted by rains, river flow, and temperature. No view of the Hoh River is complete without an understanding of this primitive calendar, a calendar never printed, but one that still guides the annual rights of passage for the hardy tribal people who settled the great rain forest of the valley.

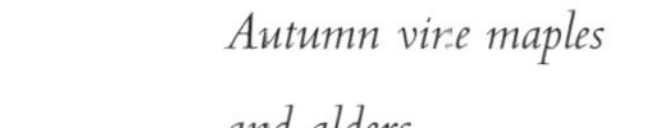

Autumn vine maples and alders

Fall – *migration and spawning*

As fall approaches, the leaves of maple and alder collect along the river shoals and the afternoon wind begins to blow briskly down the Hoh Valley. The mornings begin to frost, and the last gasp of warm breath of Indian summer is exhaled—the proverbial calm before the storm. In mid-October the fall rains arrive wet and powerful. Like monsoons, the storms will pound the coastline for two weeks. Eroding clay banks will turn the main-stem Hoh a turbid gray, and river levels will rise several feet. The tributaries will run tannin, stained dark and dreary, exceeding their banks and spreading into the riparian forest floor. Nothing is sheltered from the downpour.

The rising stream levels trigger two key events in the salmon life cycle: adult spawning and juvenile migration. With the rains, the impatient adult chinook and coho salmon begin upstream migration, silvery and fat from their marine journey. The last of the coastal cutthroat will abandon their summer holding pools and move into tributaries to stage for their spawning in winter and spring. The secretive bull trout, spurred on by the decreasing water temperatures, will move far upstream into the headwaters of the main-stem rivers. These high waters also trigger the movement of juvenile salmon and trout from their summer rearing habitats to their winter refuges, found in the smaller tributaries and floodplain streams and ponds where more stable food and safe shelter can be found.

Winter – *torrents, silver, and darkness*

Winter is a long season in the Hoh River Valley. The rainstorms of fall will continue for months, and the prolonged drenching can evoke the Fort Clatsop winter that mired the hopes of Lewis and Clark in 1805-1806. Humidity and mist are omnipresent. No place is dry. This is the time of torrents.

The winter season is the domain of the wild and mighty steelhead. This is well noted in the tribal history of the Olympic Peninsula. These powerful and prized fish enter the Hoh River as the fall chinook and coho runs trickle to a finish. They will enter over a period of six months or more and spawn well into spring and even early summer. This protracted spawning period ensures that some portion of the population always survives the winter floods.

Decaying chum salmon in alder leaves

Spring – *growth and outmigration*

As the short spring season arrives, the ebb and flow of drenching showers is accompanied by warming sun breaks that provide a period of growth, which will carry the fish through summer. The exaggerated perturbations of winter stream flows and big incoming steelhead are reduced to a rolling orchestra of pulsing flows, swarms of little emergent salmon, and a dewdrop carpet of green. Perhaps no season is more important to the annual cycle of salmon.

Spawning steelhead are ubiquitous in the shallow riffles and tailouts of long runs. Enormous silvery-sided spring chinook push their way into the main-stem Hoh River. The thick-bodied chinook will move into deep pools where they will hold until they move to their spawning grounds in late summer. The surviving juvenile salmon and trout parr that were hatched the previous year will experience the most rapid growth rates of the salmon calendar over the next few months. Some individuals will double their weight and fat stores. This growth is critical to their survival across the summer and into the fall.

River and alders in spring light

By late spring many juveniles will sense the genetic instinct to migrate downstream through the Hoh River and out into the ocean. These fish are "smolts" and they will undergo a metamorphosis that prepares them for their saltwater journey.

Spring is when the cycle for the next generation starts anew.

SUMMER – *feast or famine*

Early summer on the Olympic Peninsula is marked by infrequent bursts of temperamental rainfall alternating with long stretches of sunny weather, warm breezes, blooming flowers, and the sweet smell of cottonwood trees in the river bottoms. The arrival of adult summer steelhead and summer chinook salmon coincides with the first early rains of summer. They both will migrate far up the main-stem river, relying heavily on canyon reaches, deep pools, and bouldery runs as staging areas. Summer steelhead won't start spawning until December and will continue through spring, spawning farther upstream than their winter counterpart. The chinook will begin to spawn during the waning months of summer. By spawning at different times, these two species can stage in similar habitats without competing for spawning areas. Only through such life-history diversity can so many species coexist within the same watershed, and fully utilize the rain-forest ecosystem.

The majority of juvenile salmon and trout parr in the Hoh River basin rear in tributaries and small main-stem floodplain streams during the summer months. The growth experienced by juvenile salmon and trout parr occupying tributaries and floodplain streams during the spring continues well into summer in most years. These summer habitats vary in terms of food supply and competition. The lucky fish that inhabit the best areas will experience substantial growth in length and weight for all of the summer.

The fleeting feast and diversity of early summer life and migration is eventually compromised by drought. Although food remains plentiful for fish, stream flows will shrink to a fraction of their former levels. The reduction in water levels will be so extreme in some streams that entire sections will go dry, leaving behind a few isolated pools to support juveniles that constitute the next run of salmon.

From the spawning splendor of fall, to the torrents of winter, to the renewal of spring, to the withering summer droughts, there is a season for everything in the Hoh River Valley. The Native Americans of the Hoh, dating to their encampments at the toe of valley glaciers during the last Ice Age, thrived in the dynamic rain-forest environment. Their adaptive culture lived with the existing land, depending on perpetuation of natural productivity. This contrasts with the Euro-American influences, where rapid and extensive land alteration and resource extraction led to the boom-and-bust cycles, with all their societal debate and conflict, so typical of the American West. Perhaps by fully understanding and appreciating the sense of time and place that is embodied in this natural calendar, we may open up to pursuing a healthier balance with nature's dwindling abundance.

The Hoh people gave meaning to the year through their observations of fish, birds, mammals, weather patterns, and stream flows. Long before the first Egyptian and Roman calendars were established, the Native American cultures developed their own set of seasons. The biological calendar predates our modern versions by thousands of years. It remains the only calendar universally understood across all native languages and cultures inhabiting the northern Pacific Rim: that of the salmon.

As I sit in my office finishing this essay, the last days of the seasonal winds are shifting to the coming year. The salmon are prepared through long-tested and proven diversity. The forest is quiet in anticipation. In the salmon calendar there is a place for everything. A time for rain. A time for sun. A time for drought. A time for death, birth, and growth. It is a calendar that provides a scale of time for human minds to reconnect to wild rivers and noble salmon that are the foundations of the oldest West Coast cultures.

South Fork Hoh in winter twilight

A Good Paddle

by Mike Hagen, Hoh River Trust

A walk with Dave Hudson (also named How-ee sha-ta, or Xaw'shata in the Quileute language), Hereditary Chief of the Hoh Tribe

I interviewed Dave shortly after power had been restored to the Hoh village after the first big storm of the season. There weren't many signs of flooding this time, though more than 14 inches of rain had fallen upriver at the ranger station. We got into his pickup and drove out to the mouth of the Hoh to talk. Unlike the week before, the river mouth was wide open. The big bar was gone, and heaps of shiny new logs were piled up on the far side of the river by the Oil City trail. The surf was still big and full of storm debris.

Dave pointed to the beach at the end of the road. "I was a kid there, where the old longhouse once stood." A brushy patch of beach berm is all that stands there now, across from an abandoned frame house. Now 53, Dave spent his early years with his grandparents Pansy Howeattle Hudson and Theodore Hudson. Pansy was the great-granddaughter of Chief Howeattle, who signed the Quinault River Treaty in 1856 for the Quileute Tribe. Her Quileute name was Sho`th-a-booth. Living in the longhouse was what started Dave on his path as a teacher of the culture and traditions of the Hoh Tribe. Elders and other community members would often visit the longhouse to celebrate events ranging from naming ceremonies to births, funerals, and potlatches, each with its own songs and dances. Stories were told, people got reacquainted, and they feasted on Native dishes.

On one side of the longhouse was the sea, where they harvested clams, smelt, and crabs. From the side facing the river, they packed their water and caught steelhead, coho, and spring and fall chinook. The back of the longhouse faced the forest, where they hunted deer and elk, and gathered berries and wood. "You don't need anything else," Dave said. His grandfather had built the longhouse for potlatches. They used canoes to haul wood and supplies because there was no road. There was great purpose in their lives.

Hoh River merges with the Pacific

Dave moved away to go to school in the 1960s but returned in 1972, "to stay put." He could have gone to college, but his strong roots pulled him back to his ancestral home. Today, Dave is the teacher of tradition and culture, mostly to the younger tribal members. "First you're the student, then you're the teacher," he said with a grin. Whoever wants to learn is welcome. Not everybody may feel the need, but for those who do, including non-Native folk, the path starts with staying clean. No drugs or alcohol, a temptation that has haunted many of the Tribes since early interaction with white settlers. And the learning starts with a good canoe paddle.

Dave was on the first modern-day Coastal Tribes canoe journey in 1976. It was a nonhosted paddle, which entailed hopping into an old wooden canoe and paddling from La Push to Neah Bay with five gallons of drinking water and some fry bread. No support boats, GPS, or satellite phones; they did it the old way. "When you paddle, you sing. It keeps you in sync and you don't notice the hard work quite so much. And you learn from the old songs and stories at the campfire at night, after a long day of paddling." Nowadays, support crews set up nightly camps, fishing boats join the canoes, and safety is number one. Though many of the old traditions and methods have changed, the whole Northwest Native American population remains part of the "canoe family."

Tribal and "canoe family" culture isn't just for Native Americans, though. Many cultures now take part. "Grab a paddle and jump in," Dave said with a grin. "By the way, here are the rules . . ." Dave's family has a history of teaching their culture to outsiders. Past elder Harry Sams taught the language, dances, and carving to a local white man from Queets, Dave Forlines. Dave Hudson's Grandmother Pansy ended up adopting Forlines as her son. The late Mr. Forlines became a famous Native artist, a Quileute elder, and a source of traditional botanical knowledge. He even refurbished the Howeattle family canoe.

Dave described how the Puget Sound Tribes look up to the Coastal Tribes that have held on to the old culture and traditions. The Puget Sound Tribes have much of the wealth, but it's shared; the Hoh Tribe receives casino income from leased machines on the I-5 corridor. The Tribe chooses not to have a casino on its land.

Hoh tribal elder Dave Hudson and his son, Dave Jr., at the mouth of the Hoh

They prefer to keep life simple: no parking lots, no bright lights at night, none of the security issues and related noise.

As the Tribal Natural Resources Department policy adviser, Dave takes his job seriously. "Our natural resources, from healthy salmon runs to big trees, this is what connects us to our past." He laments that there are no longer enough large red cedar trees for dugout canoes built in the traditional way. The Tribes have had to introduce some modern techniques into their canoe building, such as fiberglass and epoxy. While out fishing on the strait, Dave met Bill Reidel, a teacher from Clallam Bay who popularized the use of cedar strip/epoxy-based boats. Dave passed this idea (and the blueprints by Conrad Taft Williams) on to the Quileute, who are now building a large paddle journey canoe out of cedar strips. Someday the Hoh Tribe may build one too, to replace their very old cedar canoe and their current fiberglass one. But Dave holds on to the dream of crafting a dugout canoe using the traditional techniques. Perhaps the big red cedars will return someday, if given the chance.